conflict management in congregations

David B. Lott, Editor

Introduction by Speed B. Leas

The Alban Institute

Scriptural quotations, unless otherwise noted, are from the New Revised Standard Version of the Bible, copyright © 1989, Division of Christian Education of the National Council of the Churches of Christ in the United States of America and are used by permission.

All the chapters in this book, except "The Basics of Conflict Management in Congregations" originally appeared in slightly different forms in *Action Information* and *Congregations: The Alban Journal*. Original copyrights © 1979, 1980, 1985, 1986, 1987, 1988, 1989, 1992, 1994, 1995, 1996, 1997, 1998 by the Alban Institute.

"The Basics of Conflict Management in Congregations" originally appeared in a different form as *A Lay Person's Guide to Conflict Management* (Bethesda: Alban, 1979). Original copyright © 1979 by the Alban Institute.

CONTENTS

Harvesting the Learnings on Conflict Management

Speed B. Leas

When Loren Mead stepped down as the president of the Alban Institute after more than 20 years as its leader, the Institute's board wisely chose Jim Wind to be its new director and guide. As part of his original mandate at Alban, Wind wanted to capture what had been learned in the years before he joined the team, and he instituted a project he called "Harvesting the Learnings." This project has had several facets, some having to do with archiving specific learnings not yet codified and some having to do with making those archives available to a new and larger public. This book, which is part of that harvest, gathers up a number of published articles and monographs written over the history of the Institute and puts them together in this more permanent and easily accessible volume for the use of present and future generations of people interested in the foundational pieces from which the reputation of the Institute was built.

The Alban Institute has had a deep interest in congregations and how they deal with conflict almost since its inception. When Loren Mead started the organization in 1974, he brought into the fold several of us who had deep and abiding interests in various aspects of congregational life. Celia Hahn, the first to join Loren at Alban, began her work helping persons interested in congregations think about clergy authority, the impact on congregations of changes in pastoral leadership, and the role of women in the church. Roy Oswald hit the ground running with his research on clergy transitions. I brought my major interest in conflict in congregations into the mix.

Before joining Alban in 1977, I had been the director of an urban training center from 1968 to 1973. It was funded by many denominations to work in Southern California on projects that would help congregations face and cope with issues of urbanization, race, justice, and the war in Southeast Asia. As director of this organization I, along with others on the staff, worked with many congregations and developed a reputation for being helpful to them. In about 1970 a pastor of a congregation in the San Diego area called us to ask for some help with a conflict not related to social concerns which had developed in that church. The conflict seemed to have started around his initiation of changes in the worship service. In recent months he had started not wearing a robe when leading worship, not using the hymnal, not having the choir sing anthems, accompanying the singing with a guitar rather than using the organ, and choosing music that sounded to some like folk and camp songs.

Two of my colleagues (Gail Visser and Paul Kittlaus) and I agreed to explore with the pastor and a number of leaders what might be done to help ameliorate some of the tensions in the congregation. We then designed this strategy: for several days we held meetings (on Saturdays and Sunday afternoons) with all of the members of the congregation who were willing to attend. The purpose of these meetings was to reduce tension in the congregation, make decisions about how worship would be conducted, and develop skills among the leaders and members of the congregation that would help them deal better with differences in the future. Much to the delight of me, my colleagues, and the vast majority of the members of the congregation, tensions were reduced. Moreover, all the members who had been active in the life of the congregation stayed (indeed, we didn't know of anyone who quit over the changes in worship or the work we did), and we got agreements about what would be done at each of the church's worship services.

Success is a great motivator! I got interested in learning more about conflict—what causes it, methods for dealing with it, and especially for ways of dealing with congregations and other voluntary systems in conflict. I began to take courses at the UCLA Graduate School of Management, at the National Training Laboratories, the Harvard Negotiation Project, and just about any other place that offered a course with the word *conflict* or *mediation* or *negotiation* in the title. I also did a lot of reading on the conflict theory that was available at the time (there wasn't much coming directly out of religious groups, denominations, seminaries, or congregations). Paul Kittlaus and I let it be known that we were available to "practice" on other congregations as well. We applied our new formal learning and what we had picked up from our congregational experience to new situations until we felt we had a pretty good grasp on both the theory and the practice of managing differences, which we then applied to congregations.

Out of that we wrote a book, *Church Fights,* which then opened many doors for us to do training and work with congregations in conflict.

In 1973 I left the urban training center in Los Angeles and joined Jack Biersdorf at the Institute for Advanced Pastoral Studies, where I began to ply my trade, full time, as one who works as a third party in conflicted congregations. Loren asked me to join the Alban Institute in 1977.

As I began to work in this area, I discovered others out there who also were curious about conflict, congregations, and what might be done to help religious people better manage the tensions of disputes, especially in a time of mainline Protestant decline. I believe this loss of institutional vigor greatly exacerbated people's feelings of being out of control and of powerlessness.

We were all struggling with how to help organizations make tough decisions, deal with antagonistic people, and cope with what seemed to be (in many places) chronic organizational dysfunction. Many of those people are represented here in this book. There was no well-trodden research path that led to understanding institutions or the grumpy people who tenanted them with any certainty. As these essays demonstrate, those who were trying to understand the phenomena of conflict in religious institutions came at the task of exploring the complexity of congregational life from a wonderfully rich variety of perspectives. Each one of them used a different instrument of analysis; each one found a "truth" which seemed dependent on their analytical approach, yet enriched and challenged what had been known previously. In this book the reader will find ideas, like those of Caroline Westerhoff, which come from a profound theological and poetic perspective on the reality in which we all live. What Caroline is able to see and say goes far beyond what those of us who emphasize other approaches are able to see. Not that she has "the truth," and the rest don't. She has a piece of "the truth," as do those whose instruments are organizational development (like Gil Rendle, Roy Pneuman, and George Parsons), as do those whose instruments are individual psychology (such as Warner White and Clinton McCoy).

Not only are each of these rich essays shaped by the intellectual perspective through which each person seeks to understand what is happening in the world, they are also profoundly influenced by the varied ways the writers went about doing research. Some of the writers are consultants and thus draw on their experience of working with individuals and groups in an outside observer/intervener role. Warner White's observations, based on his experience as an insider comparing what happened to him as a pastor in different situations, are different from those of the consultants who experience the conflict with somewhat less investment in the outcome. (Note, however, that the consultants have as much of a stake in the outcome as do the insiders. Although they may have a degree of neutrality, their stake in a successful outcome, their reputation, and the demonstration of their theories on how conflict is managed hardly puts them in a position that is either impartial, neutral, or disinterested.) Each of these authors brings differences to their writing based not only on role, but also based on culture. Ernest Walker writes from the perspective of an African American, Virstan Choy from the perspective of a Chinese American, and Margaret Bruehl uses her experience of studying mediation in China as another cultural view of conflict and how one deals with it.

What we have here is a collection of writings from people who are field researchers, each of whom brings his or her experience with a different culture and a different literature that shapes the way she or he views the world. Each one operates out a different theological understanding and has a different experience with conflict. Does one have it "right," and another not? I doubt it. Each has looked at a part and none was able to describe the whole.

One reason for that inability is that we use one word—*conflict*—to describe many different experiences and situations, but each of the experiences so named are not all the same. Some of the situations have to do with solving problems with people who are relatively secure. Some have to do with managing organizational tensions that have to do with power sharing and dispersal. Others have to do with the flawed and unpredictable ways different people cope with stress. And other experiences we call conflict are an overwhelming amalgamation of all of the above.

As I read these essays, in preparation for writing this introduction, I did not find them to be dated or passé; I found them to be fresh and immediately useful to what is confronting synagogues and churches today. Although the original pieces contained some anachronistic references to events and issues that are not the headlines of today, the dilemmas and behaviors of those in congregational leadership are poignantly contemporary.

WHAT IS SUCCESS IN MANAGING CONFLICT?

As helpful and current as these essays are, one thing that the reader will not find here is a guarantee of success in conflict management, or even a common understanding or description of *how* one might define success. Over the years of working with congregations in conflict, I have not experienced universal success with the people I have tried to help—far from it (as is certainly the case with each of the writers in this book). Indeed, this dilemma of trying to define "success" is one of the most significant problems one has in working with conflicted organizations. Sometimes people define success as making the tensions go away. Other times they define it as getting what *they* want; other times they define it as making the best possible decision under the circumstances.

The way we describe success has a profound impact on the way we go about and assess our conflict work. I recently spoke with a reporter from the *Stockton Record* who insisted on asking questions like this: "Don't you think it is a shame that religious people have conflict?" "Are religious conflicts worse than secular conflicts?" "Aren't people who go to church and then find themselves in conflict hypocrites?" He knew better than to ask these questions, everybody does, but what he was doing was expressing his disappointment that people have pain, that agreements about important things are often difficult (sometimes impossible) to find. Indeed, agreement is often difficult to find even about trivial things. He would have liked to have had an organization somewhere that does it right, that is truly a foretaste of a world we do not yet know. But, alas, though the church may give us some glimpses from time to time of what the communion of the saints might be, it falls far short of the glory to which we aspire.

In an attempt not to get caught in the trap of over-glorifying what is possible in dealing with human relationships (in congregations or other places), over the years I have tried to use the following standards to assess what success is in the conflicts with which I work:

- People were able to make decisions that stuck 18 months after the decisions were made.
- There was a significant reduction in tension.
- People used better problem-solving (conflict management) strategies in the future—at least for the next 18 months.
- If there were there losses of members, the numbers were regained within the next 18 months.

Using these ways of thinking about conflict, my success rate has been as follows:

- 42 percent of the time the congregation with which I have been working has made *some* progress on *all* of the criteria.
- 22 percent of the time the congregation made *some* progress on *some* of the criteria—in other words, they may have made a decision, but the tension continued, or member losses were not regained.
- 28 percent of the time no progress was made on any of the criteria.
- 8 percent of the time the conflict got worse—in the sense that decisions did not get made, tensions increased, and losses to the system were great.

So, one important learning for me is that I do not have the magic to produce success rates of "most of the time," or 90 percent, or other overly optimistic hopes. This, of course, is only how I assess my work; others may do significantly better. I have not seen statistics from other conflict consultants' work. Moreover, I don't know whether this "batting average" is better than "no treatment." I have no way of comparing what happens in congregations with which I work to what happens in congregations that have not brought in an outside consultant to help deal with the issues. What we have in these statistics, then, are anecdotal reports from clients who *think* that the interventions I did were significant in getting better results than we might have otherwise achieved—but this cannot be proven.

Notice that describing success in this way means "compared to something else." Success is not measured in terms of 100 percent; it is not measured in terms of either/or, conflict or no conflict. Success has to do with a degree of improvement in a difficult situation. Two authors, Bush and Folger, define "success" in terms of *empowerment* and *recognition*.[1] People who are in conflict typically are unsettled, confused, fearful, and uncertain of what to do, which results in their feeling vulnerable and out of control. Such feelings need to be countered by a sense of empowerment, by which the authors mean helping the disputing parties (1) understand what they want and why such goals are important; (2) become aware of what their options are and their ability to exercise those choices; (3) to build skills in conflict resolution; (4) develop awareness of resources to help them achieve their goals and implement creative solutions; and (5) make informed, conscious decisions about possible solutions.

At the same time, people in conflict situations become defensive and suspicious—sometimes even hostile—and focus on protecting themselves because they feel threatened and attacked by the words and behavior of the other party. When this happens, people need to find a way to look beyond their own needs to achieve what Bush and Folger call "recognition." People achieve recognition when they (1) are secure enough to consider in some reflective, appreciative way the other party's situation; (2) develop an actual desire to acknowledge the other's situation; (3) can view the situation in a more sympathetic manner; (4) acknowledge this changed perspective to the other; and (5) try to make concrete accommodations to produce a mutually satisfactory solution.

Perhaps Bush and Folger have it right. One should not even be concerned with whether or not people in a conflict are able to make decisions and "settle" their differences. Perhaps one should only measure success in terms of whether the parties to the conflict experienced empowerment and were able to "recognize" their opponent. Taking this perspective on success not only helps the consultant evaluate his or her own work, however. Speaking in terms of empowerment and recognition can also assist disputing parties evaluate the necessity of bringing in a third party to help resolve their situation and ease the pain that all involved in conflict invariably experience.

DOES ONE NEED A CONSULTANT TO DEAL WITH ALL CONFLICT?

One of the questions often asked of Alban consultants has to do with whether congregations can handle conflicts without the use of a consultant. The obvious answer is, "Of course they can. They do it all the time." The basic assumption that we make at Alban is not that one needs a consultant to manage conflict better. We assume that there are things that can be done to reduce tension and help people make better decisions. The sources for discovering and implementing those "things that can be done" certainly can come from within the congregation experiencing the conflict, from helpful denominational officials, from neighboring clergy, from secure and perceptive church or synagogue leaders—as well as from a plethora of other sources.

Certain factors, however, can have an impact on the ability of congregations to deal with the conflict. Here are some common factors that enhance the probability that it will be difficult for the congregation to manage the conflict without the help of someone who is from outside the congregation:

- Instead of dealing with the problem early, the leaders wait too long before bringing the attention of the system to dealing with the problem.
- The leaders overfocus on certain individuals or groups as culpable and chose to deal with the culpability first through shaming, punishment, or removal rather than reform or providing an opportunity to operate differently.
- The leaders of the congregation have little experience with conflict management strategies that focus on tactics other than shaming, punishment, or removal.

WHY IS CONFLICT SO DIFFICULT?

All of this often implies that if one just does it right, success will be at hand. It needs to be emphasized here that conflict is *difficult*. We are talking about something here that easily escalates and that strikes fear in the hearts of most of us. Conflict is very difficult to deal with because one rarely knows how others (especially groups) will respond to any given stimulation. One may be able to temper (manage, control) his or her responses—though even this is difficult for most of us—but truly predicting what the response of the other will be is next to impossible.

A lot of "stuff" on management and leadership out there in magazines and in bookstores leaves the strong impression that someone has figured out exactly how to deal with conflict, and that anyone can succeed at managing it. All you need to do is follow three, seven, or 25 steps and you'll no longer have trouble with difficult people or differences can be made to lose their gut-wrenching power. Most of us know, in some parts of our selves, that conflict isn't easy, though other parts of our selves hope it can be— well, if not easy—quickly and permanently resolved.

This is how it is with conflict: it is sometimes easy and sometimes very difficult, sometimes it takes a long time to diminish, it sometimes seems too easy to start (even when you don't mean to start it). Sometimes it's hard to tell when it starts, or who started it, or who has done the most to contribute to the difficulty. Conflict frequently has a deep and profound impact on everyone who plays a role in it—and I don't mean just those directly involved. Conflict not only worries those within it, it worries those who are outside of it as well. It makes them anxious or, sometimes, stimulates them. There is something enjoyable about watching other people struggle. Perhaps we feel superior to those who have gotten caught in a power struggle. They seem to look foolish and vulnerable as they struggle, and we may gain some pleasure or feel a slight disdain for those who are caught up in conflict.

Moreover, there seems to be something satisfying in seeing someone standing up to a "foe" and seeing those we perceive to be bad guys or gals struggle or be defeated. (Whether this is soul satisfying or superficially satisfying, I am not certain. It's probably more the latter in that winning and losing is usually ephemeral while that which has to do with character and growth has a lasting quality.)

Even those who are in the struggle as so-called third parties are also profoundly affected by what is going on between the parties. In my experience as a third party it is not possible to be entirely neutral in a conflict. Oh, I can usually stay neutral with regard to the outcome of the dispute (Will this person remain in her position? Will this congregation use more contemporary music in its worship?). But I find it more difficult to remain neutral about attacks on *me* and *my* integrity (people in conflict rarely confine their attacks just to the parties to the conflict) or about punitive and mean-spirited behavior directed at persons I have come to respect and enjoy (especially if they play by the rules).

One of the most powerful realities about conflict in its most difficult manifestations is that it leaves us all feeling soiled—on-lookers (outside the organization or relationship), insiders who have not taken a position and don't want to, protagonists, antagonists, and even those who will join the family or group or congregation after "it" is over. Those who raised the issues in the first place may have thought they were doing a "good deed" (it's dirty business but someone has to do it), but they usually end up feeling besmirched and angry.

I worked in a congregation in Michigan where a coterie of men had decided that the pastor was playing golf more than he was ministering to the flock, that he was claiming inappropriate expenses on his church credit card (he believed those expenses had been approved by the board), and that he was not doing anything to help the church deal with its financial difficulties. So they went to the pastor and asked him to leave quietly. They told him they would help him get a nice severance package, this would not go on his record, and the church would not have to endure any embarrassing conflict. Well, the pastor took umbrage at what he perceived to be deceitful and clandestine behavior on the part of a cabal, and he placarded the sins of this small group to the congregation and community. The charges of improper behavior and indecent motives flew back and forth. At some level each side was telling a painful truth and it deeply embarrassed everyone. At another level the truth told by each side was so exaggerated it also convicted those who spoke it of self-righteous malignance. Dirt was there, dirt was manufactured. Dirt flew.

The people who put themselves forward to deal with this conflict were not the only ones besmirched by what was happening. The neutrals in the church were uneasily self-conscious when they were in the community and others asked about what was going on at the church. At church they felt that some of their friends thought less of them for not taking their side. Even those who came to the church years after the conflict was over would experience a degree of "our" shame for the time when "we" were not able to deal with important and difficult issues in our church and "things got out of hand."

Not only does conflict besmirch us when it reaches a certain level, most of us lose our ability to think clearly and rationally. Most of us aren't very good at dealing with conflict and we don't want to go through the pain of developing those skills. Therefore, instead of functioning rationally, we overfocus on our own personal ends and on self-protection. We lose our ability to see complexity; we oversimplify; we become hyper-vigilant—looking for any sign of threat and reacting out of proportion to the amount of danger actually present. Instead of feeling powerful in conflict, most of us feel powerless and find ourselves using means that we know aren't kosher, but we don't feel completely in control of the situation.

Actually, there is nothing intrinsically bad about conflict. It is a fact of life, and often an important ingredient in making possible new ideas, new ways of doing things, and new or renewed relationships. Nonetheless, because of the real risks that we are facing and because of the way we feel about conflict in our culture, a pall or blemish or "smell" always accompanies conflict. People become skittish, fearing they may be marked or handicapped by the experience. They fear they may lose something of value— not only money or property, but perhaps their self-respect, their naïve good will, their progress and momentum toward important goals and objectives.

This is not to say that there isn't value that may come from conflict. Challenge and encounter, even when accompanied by significant loss, can leave an organization stronger. They can put to rest distorted or misleading assumptions about a matter that has never been tested, stimulate and excite lethargic groups, and even stop injustice, redress wrongs, and rebalance power that has lost restraint.

With all of the good that can come from engaging in conflict (even low levels of conflict), we know it is (or can become) dangerous stuff. Engaging in the challenge of inappropriate behavior, redressing an imbalance of power, perhaps arousing a need for change in a system that has lost its adaptive edge, may have real value for the many (or for the whole). But the danger always exists that the challenger will be caught up in the anxiety of the challenge and lose accurate perspective of the level of threat, the value of what the other has contributed, not to mention decorum and restraint. The savior becomes the tyrant.

All of this is further complicated by the fact that in conflict each move is always a judgment call. One almost never has certainty either about his or her position or about the consequences of his or her action in the midst of a dispute. When one is fishing and uses a three-pound test filament on which to attach a hook, one can be fairly certain that stressing that filament with two pounds of fish is not likely to break the leader. But one does not have that certainty when working with people (especially people under stress). Yesterday a person was able to take three pounds of stress, but I know that six months ago only one pound of stress sent him into a tirade. What side of the bed did he get up on this morning? I wonder what her reaction will be to this challenge? And what will be the reaction of others who are observing the conflict (from within the organization or outside)? Sometimes those outside the conflict are more traumatized than those within it. Their anxiety stimulates that of the insiders and so frightens them that the conflict escalates to proportions that are beyond the ability of the insiders to manage.

Because of the multiplicity of factors that will have an impact on the course of a conflict, one cannot safely and predictably say such things as

- "If they just communicate with each other, the conflict will go away."
- "When I explain the weakness of her argument, I am sure she will change her mind."
- "When I show him how much power I have, the costs of continued

conflict with me, and that resistance is futile, he will back down and go along with my proposals."

- "If I use collaborative problem-solving strategies and allow others to save face this time, they will not take advantage of my good will and continue to build up their arsenal of weapons, because they will feel safe with me."

Because we can't have any certainty that what we do will reduce conflict or produce justice (on our part or that of those we are challenging), this introduction, along with the rest of the essays in the book, is offered with a sense of diffidence and humility. What I and the other writers propose here are not answers; this is not a how-to manual. Rather, what is being explored here is the proposition that learning more about what has happened to others perhaps will help us judge better what we do with ourselves and perhaps better understand others in similar situations. Even others' "failures" may have a salvific quality for us as we think about what might have been done differently or what we might do differently in a situation with similar characteristics.

Perhaps the greatest value of this book can be that the reader will have more options in conflict. She or he will discover some ideas or choices not thought of before and may feel less trapped than when the previous catalogue of options seemed not to include acceptable actions.

Finally, a value of this book can be that we will see that others have met challenges and have coped with what was presented to them. Their coping may not always have been graceful, and it may not have provided the greatest good for the greatest number. But it may demonstrate for the reader that some responses to conflict are better than others, and it is not always the case that the most aggressive or the meanest (both in the sense of the most base and the most spiteful) will win the day.

NOTE

1. Baruch Bush, Robert A., and Joseph P. Folger, *The Promise of Mediation: Responding to Conflict through Empowerment and Recognition* (San Francisco: Jossey Bass, 1994).

PART ONE

The Dynamics of Conflict

CHAPTER 1

When Conflict Erupts
in Your Church

An Interview with Speed B. Leas

What do people fight about in churches?
People sometimes say that fights are just interpersonal or personality conflicts and that they're not substantive. I don't believe that's quite true. In my work with the Alban Institute, I've found that about half the time congregations are in conflict over issues that are important to the clergy and laity. One thing they fight about is values. They have conflict over liturgy, social action, theology, and lifestyle issues.

Congregations have conflict over other noninterpersonal problems, too. For example, if people aren't doing their jobs, or they don't know how to do them adequately, conflict often develops.

About 46 percent of the time we encounter situations that do have a high degree of interpersonal difficulty and emotional conflict.

How do serious conflicts get started in a parish?
Usually people get ahold of clues that they have differences. They realize their values are different; they feel they're not getting the attention or recognition that they need. They discover style differences. Often these are not dealt with while they're still small problems.

People will then begin to collect a bagful of these slights and hurts. When they get enough in the bag, they will do something that precipitates a confrontation: they'll call the bishop or circulate a petition; the choir will walk out; people will attempt to change the slate of nominees for a certain office.

It's at this point that people usually think, "Oh, this is a big fight. This is terrible. We're out of control." Now they will address the problems.

Conflict is a part of everyday life. How can you tell when you're in the midst of a serious conflict that will require some special attention?
How do you know how bad it is? The Alban Institute has done a good deal of research over the years. On the basis of observing behavior in conflicts, I differentiate five levels of conflict. The objectives and the language of the people in the conflict distinguish the different levels. The first two levels are easy to work with; the third is tough; the fourth and fifth are very difficult and impossible.

In the first level of conflict the people who are in disagreement will stay focused on the problem. Their language will be specific and clear. They are problem solving and not feeling panicked.

In level two conflict, people become much more self-protective. In fact, self-protection will become their first agenda; the problem itself will become the second. They will also begin to use very general language and not talk specifically about an issue. They'll talk about trust and communication. None of those words means anything until you find out who's not communicating with whom, or what kind of nontrusting behavior has occurred.

In the third level of conflict, people turn from self-protection and become more interested in winning, that is, getting their position sustained in the organization. They will want to get people elected, for example, or have their position adopted by the organization. Their language begins to distort matters rather dramatically. Their talk reveals that they view the world dichotomously. They talk about us and them; they begin to see others as malevolent in their intentions. They become expert mind readers. They talk about perceptions as if they were facts.

In level four conflict, the objectives of the people involved change again. Folks are no longer interested in just winning. They are trying to get rid of someone. They feel there has to be a divorce: the pastor has to leave. Language becomes even more distorted.

In level five conflict, people become religious fanatics about their position. They feel themselves called by God to eradicate from the earth those to whom they are opposed. The pastor must not be simply fired; he must be prevented from getting another church. Or if he is called by another parish, that congregation must be warned.

When is an outside person helpful in the management of conflict?
At level three. At lower levels of conflict, people aren't hurting enough to
know they need help. They aren't motivated enough to work with an
outsider to deal with their differences. An outsider can, however, train people
in conflict management skills when they're involved in the lower levels of
conflict.

Dramatic, public, precipitating events are good in that they do galva-
nize the organization. They wake it up. And that's often just what's needed,
even if people don't like it when it happens. At least then they're motivated
to work on the problem.

*Are there behavior patterns that fuel a conflict and prevent construc-
tive resolution from occurring?*
I've already talked about the role of language that people use with one
another. Another common behavior pattern is also debilitating—withdrawing from one another. Instead of talking with people with whom they disagree, people talk only to those they think will agree with them. They organize themselves into clusters of like-minded people.

Also, people use information that is made up, that is, they *guess* about
people's intentions and actions. All of these behavior patterns exacerbate
the conflict.

*It's hard to get even two people who are angry with each other to
resolve their differences. How can a large group of people ever hope
to do it? Are there ground rules that facilitate groups working together
under high stress?*
There certainly are. One of the key ones is to help everybody who is going
to be involved in dealing with the differences set up the process that will be
used to work through the problems. They must believe the process will be
fair, that they will have ample opportunity to influence the outcome. An
environment of safety needs to be clearly developed, too. Making a safe
environment includes setting up clear ground rules about how people are
going to deal with each other. It includes talking about what different decision-making processes will be used. It includes agreeing not to engage in
threatening behavior and talk.

It is important to recognize that issues *are* important—even though
some people involved will deny it. It takes a lot of work to define a problem
and talk about it specifically. Even naming the issues is frightening.

What different decision-making processes can people use when trying to resolve their differences?

The way I prefer people in organizations to make decisions is collaboration. Everybody who is affected by the problem is brought into the arena where the problem will be worked on. No decision is made until the vast majority of the people agree. Everyone works together; they pool their energy and share information to find the solution that is best for everyone.

If the group isn't able to collaborate, negotiation is a second way to make decisions. We trade off with one another: I'll give you this if you give me that. Everyone should get as much as possible, but no one will get everything.

If collaboration and negotiation fail, then people have to move into the authority system of the organization. Sometimes that means voting or sometimes a certain official makes the decision.

There are other ways to make decisions, too. You can *avoid* making a decision. That means that the status quo remains. That in itself is a decision. If people can't make decisions, they won't be able to work out their differences. They will remain stuck in their dissatisfaction. Of course, people must have a clear understanding of what the problem is in order to make clear decisions.

Are there basic attitudes or assumptions that are essential to successful conflict management?

An optimistic determination. You've got to believe that it's possible to find a mutually satisfying solution. And you have to set yourself to do the hard work of trying to get that solution. Mutually satisfying decisions don't come easily. They certainly don't come out of a sweetness-and-light or a Walt Disney approach to the world.

It is essential, too, to set realistic goals for your management of conflict. I have four that I focus on: The first is to help people define clear decisions that they can make. Second, I want to help them join in decision-making processes that are fair and legal. Everyone needs a chance to participate appropriately.

My third goal is to reduce tension within the organization. I want to help people not be so frightened, so that when they come into the arena where they are making decisions, they can bring their best selves. If I can help minimize their fears, they can think more clearly and contribute positively and usefully to the conversation. Finally, I want to help people learn from the conflict itself. They can learn conflict management techniques—what works and what doesn't.

This interview originally appeared in Soundings, *the magazine of the Episcopal Diocese of Minnesota, and was conducted by Susan K. Henderson, the magazine's interim editor at the time. It later was reprinted in* Action Information *11, no. 5 (September/October 1985): 16-17, to promote Speed Leas's then-new and still-available publication,* Moving Your Church through Conflict *(Bethesda: Alban, 1985).*

CHAPTER 2

The Basics of Conflict Management in Congregations

Speed B. Leas

"I thought the church was different from other organizations—especially with regard to conflict," a confused and depressed lawyer once said to me. His church's vestry was in the midst of a painful and protracted battle with the school board that ran their parish day school. He went on to say that he had joined the church hoping that he would learn to live with others in a more fruitful way—more profoundly influenced by the gospel. He said, "The church should be special; there should be more forgiveness here; people ought to try harder to express love and care for one another. It seems like we have failed at all that."

Surely this attorney's hope speaks for most of us: we want the church to be a unique community where the fruits of the spirit are manifest in its life. Sometimes the church falls short of that dream, however, and wishing it would be better won't make it so. Committed Christians, when they find themselves in a situation of conflict, know that it must be faced squarely and that Christ's words to us inform the way we treat those with whom we disagree. More than that, the Gospel accounts, the book of Acts, and the epistles are constant reminders that this hoped-for community was often just as elusive for the early Christians as it is for us.

My theological understanding is that the church hopes for more than other institutions. At the same time, the church trains its members—by their life together in a Christian community that has the same problems as other organizations—to use methods that are both Christian and effective (1) to deal with interpersonal and organizational strife and (2) to reflect on their behavior in conflict beyond the dynamics of temporal winning and losing.

I am writing this for people who care about the church but are not paid to keep it going. Clergy and other paid staff often find it difficult to be helpful managers of conflict in a disrupted situation because their high stake in the solution to the problems prompts them to function as an advocate rather than as a facilitator. Further, the clergyperson is often the one about whom the rest of the organization is fighting. The pastor finds it difficult, if not impossible, to get and keep enough distance to be helpful as the leader of the process for healing unless it happens on his or her terms.

I am writing this for senior wardens, church moderators, congregation presidents, and lay leaders who find their congregation in conflict and want to have some ideas about what they can do about it. I want to be as practical as possible here so that the reader will be able both to understand the problems of the organization and to have a clear idea about what to do about those problems.

What Is Conflict?

Anatol Rapoport, in his book on conflict, distinguishes between "Fights," "Games," and "Debates."[1] Each represents a level of conflict. In a *debate* the objective is to convince one's opponent to see things according to one's own perspective. In a *game* the object is to outwit the other, and perhaps an audience, in order to come out as the victor. In both games and debates the opponent is an essential ingredient. In a debate, changing the opponent is the goal. In a game, says Rapoport, "a strong opponent is valued more than a weak one. In a way, therefore, the opponents in the game cooperate. First they cooperate in the sense of following absolutely and without reservation the rules of the game. Second, they cooperate in 'doing their best,' that is, in presenting to each other the greatest possible challenge. The challenge is what makes the game worthwhile."[2]

In a *fight*, however, the opponent is mainly a nuisance. He or she should not be there, but somehow there the person is. The opponent "must be eliminated, made to disappear, or cut down in size or importance. The object of a fight is to harm, destroy, subdue, or drive away the opponent."[3]

In the local church, as long as we stay within the realms of cooperation, games and, yes, even debates, we usually remain confident that we are not in conflict. When we move into the realm of fighting, however, the fear and irrational behavior begin to escalate. As long as we're debating or contesting at the game level, people feel comfortable and perhaps even exhilarated by the give and take of organizational life. For example, when the congregation is debating the merits of a new building, people are not necessarily threatened or concerned about differences of opinion and attempts to sway others' opinions—until someone threatens to quit if things don't go his or her way. There is no particular discomfort, until someone attacks the motives and legitimacy of the participation of certain individuals in the discussion, until groups begin to challenge the right of others to be leaders or to belittle their attempts to be in positions of leadership.

We have entered the realm of disruptive and painful conflict when the congregation has moved from debates and games to fighting. Within the organization one key clue that this has happened is when people no longer calculate their remarks to edify or change others, but plan them (often unconsciously) to hurt, demean, defame, or destroy the other. Other clues that we are in the midst of a fight are: (1) when we begin to be uncertain whether our relationships will be able to weather the storm of difference; (2) when we feel rejected by people who were our friends; (3) when we feel we have no control over the development and testing of the organization; and (4) when the pain of competition is greater than the exhilaration of challenge.

We are in a fight when accusations are made and it seems that the "others" want to destroy the church or split it down the middle. People pepper their conversation with words that have violent connotations: aggressive, devastate, annihilate, abuse, molest, ruin, vicious, thoughtless, and so on. The words become grandiose and reveal hidden fears of violence, destruction, and loss of control.

We are not in a situation of serious conflict as long as (1) the participants feel confident that they will be able to manage the differences that are there; (2) the decision-making processes authorized in the church constitution and by-laws stay firm and are used; (3) the people operate within the specifically stated and generally understood rules of appropriate behavior in the church; and (4) the people are willing to cooperate in processes suggested by the leadership groups.

WHAT DO PEOPLE FIGHT ABOUT?

People in congregations fight about just about everything you can imagine. Over the years I have worked with local churches having serious conflicts over such things as: whether young people should sleep coeducationally in tents on a church retreat; whether women should be ordained to the priesthood; whether people may speak in tongues in the 11:00 A.M. worship service; whether the new organ should be placed in the front or back of the sanctuary; how much time per week the pastor spends calling; how large a new building to erect; whether to change the prayer book; how to deploy church benevolences; and which biblical scholars should be taken seriously with regard to scriptural inerrancy.

More often than any of the above issues, however, the most common question is "Shall we retain Reverend So-and-So as our pastor?" This question seems to arise with equal frequency, regardless of a church's polity; whether the judicatory or the congregation makes the final decision seems to matter little. Congregations most frequently experience conflict over the pastor's tenure. By and large, other church controversies tend to stay in the realms of games and debates, but leadership questions quickly become fights.

Moreover, the fights about whether or not the pastor should stay seem to be the least focused and specific. I once worked with a very typical congregation in the midst of a fight. Fifty-five percent of the congregation wanted the pastor to stay, 45 percent wanted him to leave. In my report to the congregation I listed the complaints against the pastor cited by the latter group: "Those who are uncomfortable with Reverend So-and-So's ministry mention most often his lack of calling on certain individuals, the fact that he speaks too softly from the pulpit, that he has worn blue jeans to the church building on Saturday, that he sometimes uses modern speech in worship, that the church office is not covered during normal business hours, and that he is not married."

Except for the matter of the pastor's marital status, these complaints are so typical of successful and unsuccessful pastors alike they sound almost like a litany. What is particularly problematic for the person who wants to help this congregation manage its differences is that the "charges" are seemingly inconsequential according to our usual societal standards and values, and those who support the pastor deride and pooh-pooh the complaints.

Casual observers who do not appreciate the importance of interpersonal relationships in a local congregation might quickly side with the pastor's supporters against those whose concerns don't seem weighty enough to bring to the court of continuing pastoral tenure. Yet what has happened is that the pastor has never been comfortable dealing with these people who have now become his enemies. He doesn't call on them as frequently or for as long as he does the others in the church. He doesn't linger with them after meetings or go out with them for a cup of coffee. He tends not to recommend them for committee assignments. In general, he is polite but distant toward this group. They have picked up the "vibes" and don't like being set apart. After five years they feel lonely and left out. They would like to have someone in the leadership position whose approbation they would receive.

When asked to justify what it is they don't like about the pastor they vainly try to find reasons. Somehow, it is not OK to say, "I don't know, I just don't like him," or "He doesn't pay enough attention to me." Consequently they come up with a list of complaints they hope will, at best, catch his attention so that he will be more aware of their presence and importance. At worst, they figure such a list may help get rid of him so that perhaps a person will come into that place who will care about and attend to them.

To answer the question, then, "What do people fight about?"—sometimes it is substantive issues, but often it is lack of recognition and the deterioration of interpersonal relationships.

WHY DO PEOPLE FIGHT?

It is obvious why people fight when we can see some specific substantive issues over which there is disagreement. Usually these substantive differences center on facts, methods, goals, or values. Differences over *facts* may have to do with definitions of the problem, acceptance or rejection of particular information as factual, or differing impressions of one's respective power and authority. Differences over *methods* may have to do with procedures, strategies, or tactics that would most likely achieve a mutually desired goal. Differences over *goals* have to do with what should be accomplished: the desirable objectives of a church, a department, or a mission project. Finally, differences over *values* concern the way power should be exercised, particularly in respect to certain moral considerations, assumptions about justice, fairness, and so on. These differences arise regularly in the course of organizational life and may be the occasion for games, debates, or fights.

There are also a variety of needs people have that do not manifest themselves in the above listing of substantive issues. Sometimes we fight because we are unsure that we are just as important or just as competent as another person. We may have the need to show others, and perhaps ourselves, that we are big and strong and important. Sometimes we try to feel worthwhile by competitively comparing ourselves with others (the way I know I'm OK is to know that at least I'm better than you).

At other times people need attention. They have been neglected too long and don't know how to ask positively and directly for notice. Instead of finding ways to seek positive regard, they avoid the loneliness of indifference through challenging and contentious behavior.

In addition to needs for attention and for power, a number of people in churches are motivated to stay in a fight out of the need for revenge. It is not unusual to find people smarting from the pain of a confidence betrayed, a trust broken, or an attack endured, who are out to pay back double those who hurt them or "let them down." Often they will not reveal their motivation easily and openly to others (or even to themselves) because they know such motives are inappropriate in the church. However, there is no question that their interest in staying in the fight is generated out of their desire to hurt those they perceive have hurt them.

WHAT DO PEOPLE DO THAT IS NOT HELPFUL WHEN THEY FIGHT IN CHURCH?

Dropouts. Some stop coming to the worship services, some to certain meetings, others stop pledging, and still others transfer their membership. Not all self-removals are a bad thing. The family that decides no longer to participate may have goals for congregational participation that this church may choose not to meet. The family may wish to participate in public affirmation of the gifts of the Spirit through charismatic worship, and this congregation is not "into" that. Or it may be that the family wants biblically fundamental preaching and the preacher is not a fundamentalist.

The pressure put on leaders and members to attract and keep all comers can be deleterious to congregational life. In order to have organizational identity, it is important to establish boundaries that help people understand what is unique and important about being a member at a particular congregation and what doesn't fit. For life and growth and enthusiasm to exist in the congregation, choices must be made as to the direction and identity of the congregation. If "everyone" is welcome probably few will feel meaningfully involved and committed to important purposes. Therefore, if people choose to leave because they feel this congregation is too liberal to meet their needs, it might be appropriate for them to find a more conservative church home.

Some dropping out, however, is premature. Some members don't challenge the system enough to give it a chance to respond better to their needs. Sometimes they drop out because they feel helpless to change or challenge the system. They go away nursing their anger or disappointment, using their energy not to improve the system but to blame themselves or others for the problems they are experiencing.

Often those who drop out prematurely are immobilized by their anger and feel helpless or hopeless to cope with the situation within the church organization. The church not only loses their financial and volunteer resources, but it also loses their perceptions and motivation to improve the situation. These perceptions might help the congregation develop to the extent that it can be more responsive to the needs of others in the future.

The decision for the conflict manager here is a difficult one. Would it be better to encourage this family to continue to participate or shall they be "allowed" to find another church home? The following questions might be helpful in assessing what to do in the case of a drop out:

- Does the individual or family cause excessive disruption when they participate?
- Is the family or individual a chronic complainer?
- Is there anything we can do or want to do about their grievance?
- Do we know why this family is not participating? Often others incorrectly ascribe motives for nonparticipation.

Blame. This is the most common conflict management problem in the local church. Somehow it seems as if the congregational members must come up with a clear, concise statement of who wears the white hats and who wears the black hats. Generalizations are made at all levels—psychological, sociological, theological, and organizational—to explain what has made the others so nasty and inept. In one church fight I witnessed half of the congregation said the other half caused the difficulties, because they were "trying to act like this is an upper-class church." Those so branded were not at a loss for a response, saying that the other group was too dependent on the pastor and couldn't think for themselves.

I have not worked in a congregation yet where, from an outside perspective, one "side" was blameless. In every case each group has participated to a greater or lesser degree in blaming the other for the problems. Further, each group sees itself as much more benevolent toward the other than is actually the case. In one church, the group who was supporting the pastor saw themselves as blameless; they only wanted to affirm their relationship to this woman whom they saw as competent and worthy to be their minister. In the very next breath, however, they went on to describe the others as cold, uptight, uncaring, and continual troublemakers in the church. "This is the very same group that assassinated two previous pastors," a member of the pastor's support group said to me.

Not only do people in conflict tend to see the opposition as more malevolent and themselves as more benevolent than they actually are, but they tend to look for simple, single causes for the organizational difficulty. It seems that they just have to have something or someone to blame. In fact, conflict almost always has multiple causes. And those causes almost never come solely from one group or one person. People who get caught in the anxiety and complexity of conflict situations find it helpful to be able to identify how each group participates in creating the difficulty. After all, each party only has control over itself. There is very little you can do to control the other people in the situation. If each group is willing to look seriously at how it causes, creates, or adds to the organizational difficulty, not only will the conflict diminish, but the possibility that an agreement may be reached becomes greater.

Attack. Character assassination is the usual mode of attack in church fights. It is implied that the pastor is lazy. It is implied that the "opposition" is led by insecure persons who are not able to handle their own family lives, and they are working out their personality disorders in the church. It is implied that the reason a certain group is opposed to the ordination of women is because of their insecurity with their own sexuality. These statements are examples of assaults church folk use to hurt, damage, discredit, or drive out their opposition. None of them is helpful.

Some things that may not be intended as attacks are experienced as such. Petitions are an example of this. Sometimes people feel that they are having a difficult time being heard and taken seriously in the local congregation. They drop hints here and there; they raise complaints in meetings; perhaps they even write a letter to the pastor or the church board and nothing happens. Finally, in an attempt to be taken seriously, they circulate a petition among some of the members of the congregation or hold a meeting in someone's home to discuss "the problem." The other group often perceives this as an attack, but it may not be. It is not an attack if:

- All the people in the church had an opportunity to see and discuss the petition before it was submitted.
- The wording of the petition is clear and specific.
- The petition asks for appropriate and possible changes.
- The petition is submitted to the proper boards and authorities within the local congregation before it goes to the judicatory.

So-called secret meetings are also sometimes seen as attacks. Again, they are not necessarily that if only one or two such meetings are held and the concerns of the people who attended the meetings are openly and completely shared with the formal boards of the congregation. When the self-appointed committee does not share its concerns or its strategies with everybody (or at least let the plans be available to those who want to know), that "committee" is probably taking a saboteur-like stance, undermining the open-trust relationships that characterize a healthy voluntary organization.

Generalizing. One of the things that makes conflict management most difficult is the tendency many have of moving too quickly from the specific to the general. Instead of saying that we don't like a person's beard, we tend to assume that the beard is a manifestation of the person's deeper psyche. Instead of naming our disappointment about the fact that the pastor didn't speak to us on the street, we identify the snub as evidence that he or she doesn't like us. Our concerns about the changes in the prayer book get generalized into a fear that the whole church is going to hell in a handbasket.

The more general the conflict, the more difficult it is to handle; conflicts over specific matters are easier to manage. Not only do our generalizations raise our fear (because we see the problem as huge and difficult), but they also make it very awkward to find a place to begin to work on the problem. If we define the problem as lack of communication, where do we start communicating? But if we define it as the fact that the pastor didn't speak to Mildred, then the action obviously indicated is to go talk to Mildred, now. If we define the problem as a lack of trust in the organization, where do we start trusting? But if we say that the treasurer doesn't share all the financial records, the trust issue is dealt with by working with the treasurer.

Often generalizations are couched in psychological jargon about the reasons for a person's or a group's behavior. This is most unhelpful. If we define the organizational problem as the pastor's unresolved authority problem with his father, what can we as laypersons do about it? Such a problem definition guarantees that we will be helpless even to begin confronting the issues. Psychological definitions of problems seem to require psychological solutions that are beyond our grasp. Defining the problems in terms of specific behaviors that are annoying, counterproductive, or a breach of contract will help us get handles on our problems, rather than generalizing the problems into realms that are beyond our control.

Distorted or interrupted communication. Although communication issues are the most often identified problems in church conflicts, I caution you that frequently people too quickly sum up organizational difficulties this way. Sometimes after people improve their communication, they find their problems only increase because they learn that there are differences even greater than they had assumed when the communication was poorer.

Nonetheless, communications are frequently the major problem. Sometimes members are afraid to tell one another what they think, especially if they don't like something, so they will tell a third party rather than the one with whom they have the difference. The third party communicates the difficulty (sometimes with an added flourish), leaving the originally aggrieved party anonymous. Now the person who hears the problem doesn't know what to do to work on the problem because he or she doesn't know who to talk to.

Consider this illustration: The Pastor-Parish Relations Committee heard rumors that an unspecified number of people were upset with the amount of visiting the pastor was doing. The PPRC didn't address the issue in a way that the unhappy people could see, though the pastor did increase her visiting. So the people with the grievance drew up a petition signed by 33 members. This so upset the pastor that she asked the district superintendent to move her the following June. This resignation infuriated the people who liked the pastor. The petition signers were perplexed; they had not intended for the pastor to resign, and they were satisfied when they heard that the pastor's calling routine had changed. In this case the pastor decided to stay in the congregation once she was able to clarify who had the grievance, the extent of the grievance, and what actions were required to satisfy the largest number of people.

Anonymous communication is usually destructive and harmful to the organization. It is always helpful to encourage all persons who have grievances to let you quote them (specifically with their name attached). It is even better to help the person share the difficulty himself or herself with those who can do something about the situation.

From time to time a pastor or lay leader will receive an anonymous letter in the mail. My advice is to ignore it; do not take it to a personnel committee, church council, or any other body. To do so would communicate to the sender that anonymous communications are taken seriously and would enhance the secret sender's influence. Further, it implies that the charges cannot be challenged by those against whom they are made. An accused person should always have the right to confront his accuser if he or she so chooses. Anonymity does not allow that option. Anonymous letters should be lost letters.

People who are afraid to have their names used or are afraid to talk to the person with whom they disagree should be thoughtfully and carefully encouraged to do their own communicating. If they are uncomfortable doing it alone, offer to go with them. If they just can't bring themselves to speak about their concern themselves, then tell them that you will share what they have told you only if you have their permission to use their name.

WHAT ATTITUDES WILL HELP YOU MANAGE THE CONFLICT?

Let us begin this discussion by remembering Jesus' attitudes toward conflict. He was not passive; he was confrontive and direct. In the Sermon on the Mount he said that when you have been struck on one cheek you should turn the other cheek. What that means to me is that when the battle has begun, I do not leave, nor do I attack. I stay there. I stay in range of getting hit again. I take the risk of not destroying the other person or leaving the scene.

Mutually acceptable solutions are available. I make the assumption that if we work at it long enough we will find a way to work things out between us. This is a faith statement; it is a statement of hope. Any relationship presupposes a commitment to a joint outcome, an agreement that each partner may have to give up a little in order to reach a solution both can live with. If I don't believe that mutually acceptable solutions are available, then why should I give up anything, or why should I allow you to interfere with my wants and needs?

If the members of your congregation don't have some sense of hope about being able to work out a solution, then people end up feeling they must either be doormats or drive those who disagree out of the organization. Often these attitudes are not thought out or stated quite as boldly as I have put them here, but the style of the battle as it is joined reveals their presence.

If you don't have any hope that a mutually acceptable solution is available to the organization, the first thing you should do is check the impressions of others both in and out of the church. They might help you see some things you had not previously thought of.

A desire to implement solutions. Not only must you perceive that solutions are available, but the members of the organization must want to implement them. What may be required may be something that neither you nor the other members would want to live with. These two perceptions regarding the availability and desirability of mutually acceptable solutions are simply another way of defining the difference between a fight and games or debates. If you see no alternatives that lead to a commitment to a joint outcome, then you are in a fight where the driving out of some will seem justified to you.

Belief in cooperation rather than competition. Alan Filley makes this point in his book, *Interpersonal Conflict Resolution:*

> There is a great deal of consistent evidence to suggest that cooperative groups are more satisfied, have greater interest in the task, are more productive, and have a better division of labor than competitive groups. . . . To illustrate: If five men are engaged in the task of climbing a mountain and are competing, each must depend upon his own knowledge of the task, physical skill, and strength in carrying his equipment. It is not likely that group members will share information about the task with each other. In a cooperative group, on the other hand, tasks can be allocated among group members according to their skills and interests. One member may have superior knowledge about the process of preparation and may lead in the planning effort; another may have superior skill in mountain climbing and may lead in that activity; another may have much greater physical strength than the others and may carry a

greater load up the mountain. Thus, cooperation can fully utilize the unique strengths of each member and can foster sharing of resources within the group.

It may be argued that intergroup competition will strengthen performance and increase cohesiveness within each individual group, and indeed, this does happen; yet after a competition between two groups, only the winning group is likely to remain cohesive and satisfied. The defeated group will become fragmented and dissatisfied, perhaps seeking an opportunity for retaliation.[4]

Statements of the opposition are legitimate descriptions of their position. How often have we heard in a conflict situation, "I don't really believe what they are saying; they are just saying that to pacify us." Sometimes the put-down of the other's statements is more subtle: "Yes, I know that they said the fact that the pastor was not married was not important to most of them, but underneath that is the main issue." If we do not believe that what other people say approximates what they think or feel or intend, communication and cooperation between the parties will be stymied. In other words, to move from a posture of fight to a posture of cooperation and collaboration, one must believe that what the others say is close to what they mean. The most important thing we can do to help in this regard is saying what we mean to others consistently (even if it is something they don't like or agree with). Then we will begin to establish a belief that at least what we say can be trusted. From that base we can move toward finding a way to join together to find mutually satisfactory solutions to our organizational difficulties.

Differences are OK. How difficult it is to come to this appreciation in a local church. The usual norm is that "to differ is to reject." This certainly does not have to be the case. Often differences are those things that open new ways to approaching difficult subjects; differences prompt people to look harder and longer at subjects and issues that they previously may have taken for granted. If you have been married more than three months you know that your spouse does not agree with you on every subject. Nonetheless, it is possible for people to differ and live together and love one another. Sometimes people "agree to disagree on certain issues." Other times they acknowledge the difference and work hard at trying to arrive at a mutually acceptable course of action that both parties find useful and meaningful. While differences can lead to fighting, they can also lead to cooperation.

I once worked with a congregation in Alabama where half of the congregation was very uncomfortable with the minister's leadership and the other half staunchly supported it. Those supporters initially assumed that members who had problems about the kind of leadership the pastor should give should leave the church. Such an assumption moves the group all the way to a fight stance even before they have tried to find a way to work with one another. As the contentious 2000 U.S. presidential election demonstrated, what a tragedy it would be if those who supported the losing candidate had to leave the country—or be quiet—because the winner was not their choice. We value a loyal opposition in national politics; we ought also to value a loyal opposition in the parish.

In this particular case I helped the members look at the possibilities for agreement rather than how to make a decision about who was going to have to leave. At first nobody believed it was possible even to consider anything but division, but after they had explored alternatives for some time they were able to come to an agreement that most of the people found to be mutually satisfactory. (Not everyone was happy with this, however; several people felt that the decision had to be all or nothing and were so disappointed that they left the church).

WHAT ARE THE GOALS OF THE CONFLICT MANAGEMENT PROCESS?

The ultimate goal of the conflict management process is to move the congregation out of the chaos and confusion of enmity into reconciliation. The hope is that we will be able to help people choose to cope with the difficult situation and to feel in charge of themselves and the organization—while not denying the right of others also to share in the control of that organization. Ultimately the goal is to move from enmity to amity, to move from malevolence to benevolence.

Many times, however, this goal is beyond our grasp, and we must settle for the penultimate rather than the ultimate. I have five penultimate goals for the conflict management process:

1. *Making clear decisions.* One of the most important steps to reconciliation is the ability of the organization to make a decision about its difficulties. Often people wait too long before making the necessary decisions, which increases pain and drags out the difficulties. Jim Glasse, formerly of

Lancaster Seminary, has pointed out to me that the words *homicide, suicide*, and *decide* all have the same root. The root *cidere* means "to cut." To decide is to cut off.

Conflict management is the art of decision making, cutting off the fight, and getting on with the business of the organization. It is stopping the battle and declaring what we will now do so that we can go back to working with one another. The first goal of conflict management, then, is to make decisions.

2. *Increasing tolerance for difference.* The task of the person working with the organization as it deals with conflict is to help the people appreciate the fact that people do differ and that isn't all bad. Opposing opinions can be helpful for clarifying problems and bringing differing levels of need to the surface.

Part of our difficulty may be that our organizational norms have told us that difference is bad and is a sign of failure. Therefore, not only is the conflict painful, but the shame that comes from breaking the rules adds to the discomfort. Help the people by regularly reminding them that difference is not necessarily bad, that this conflict may bring good results—in the long run—and that perhaps we can learn from and be enriched by the opinions of others.

3. *Reducing aggression.* The conflict manager will also want to make clear that behavior directed at hurting, belittling, destroying, or getting rid of others is not helpful. Much more useful is behavior aimed at changing or improving others or, at least, stopping behavior on their part which is hurting or harmful to you.

You may ask about the need on some occasions to dismiss a pastor from his or her position; doesn't this require aggressive behavior? Not necessarily. Although such an action on the part of an official board may indeed be experienced as aggressive by the person whose position is being terminated. But if the board is clear that the relationship is not working and that it is in the best interest of all parties concerned, then such action is not necessarily aggressive. When it is a carefully planned and loving act, in the best interest of all, then it is not aggressive.

4. *Reducing passive behavior.* Quitting, "going limp," or withdrawing is not helpful behavior because it does not allow the groups or individuals to join in a collaborative effort to find a mutually acceptable solution. Even if the passive person "goes along" with the decision, the commitment will be weak and the relational bonds will more likely be insecure than would be the case if the person or group spoke up and participated in the conflict.

5. *Reducing covert, manipulative behavior.* This goal is almost the same as the one above. Both behaviors imply secret commitments not to go along with the other group or groups. The whole purpose of conflict management is to get joint decisions. Manipulative behavior produces only a forced decision with which the other may comply but to which it is unlikely there will be commitment.

Take, as a hypothetical example, St. Mary's in Middletown, a small congregation with 250 members and one priest. A group of people in that parish are very active in the Cursillo Movement and are putting pressure on others in the congregation who have not made their retreat or become "cursillistas." The non-Cursillo people are not comfortable with the cursillistas, who are now meeting regularly for meetings after their experience, and dislike continually being asked to go on a Cursillo retreat. The Cursillo people want the church to sponsor an outreach program to young people in the community. The church has a gymnasium and they'd like a lot of the people in the community to come in and use it so they'd have more young people in the church. Non-Cursillo people are opposed to the idea; they're afraid that their building is going to be wrecked. They don't want to support the Cursillo people and they feel very uncomfortable. They feel put down by the cursillistas who seem to act superior because of a special spiritual experience.

The ultimate goal that we conflict managers might have for the rector, the vestry, and the people in that congregation, obviously, is one of reconciliation where these groups move from estrangement to friendship, from enmity to amity. It is unlikely we'll get that immediately; we shouldn't even expect that in 12 months. We can expect some penultimate things to occur there, however, which will be the goals of our work. We can help people identify a number of issues about which decisions need to be made. We can talk, for example, about how and when cursillistas are to be recruited. We can talk about whether a teen program should be instituted in the church and, if so, what kind of program it should be. Those decisions can be made in that organization and they can be made fairly soon, with the full participation of all those who would be affected by the decisions. So our job is going to be to encourage people to state their concerns openly (there's a lot more talk about that right now in the parking lot and on the telephone than there is in vestry meetings). We will want to get the informal communications systems at St. Mary's congruent with the formal communications systems. We will talk in vestry meetings about the same things they talk about in the parking lot. We will help both sides recognize the validity of each other's views, and help them feel strong in stating their positions without compromising them in the initial stages of decision making. We will move directly and deliberately to find those formal channels within the organization for making the decisions. These are the goals of the conflict management process.

WHAT CAN YOU DO TO HELP MANAGE CONFLICT?

Decision-making strategies. The first, and most important thing a lay leader can do to help manage conflict in the church is to figure out how to help the official board make decisions. There are five possible strategies the board can use: collaboration, negotiation, voting, hierarchy, and avoiding.

Collaboration is the best way to make decisions. The results will more likely be fully "owned" by all parties and they will have higher commitment to follow through. By collaboration we mean co-laboring, making decisions by consensus. That is, the decision is not final until virtually everybody understands what is going on, joins in the problem solving, and agrees with the solutions at which they arrive.

Collaboration is the most difficult and time-consuming decision-making strategy. Often it is stressful, agonizingly slow, and risky under threatening circumstances. Often, in conflict, the parties feel the risks of collaboration are too great and assume the process would take too long so they turn to less costly strategies (and get what they pay for).

Collaboration requires a faith that it will be possible to find and arrive at not only a mutually satisfactory solution but also a process that includes ample opportunity and time to explore fully the problem and possible solutions. Usually, people in voluntary organizations aren't willing to pay this price, because it requires more than they previously have been used to giving. Therefore, they often move prematurely to voting or to other hierarchical decision-making modes.

How does one collaborate in a highly stressful setting? These things are necessary:

- Clear ground rules
- Agreement as to who will participate
- Ample time to work through issues
- The participation of all key leaders

- Clarity as to the process to be used
- A hope that the group will be able to find a mutually satisfactory solution

Consider this illustration of such a process. Half the leadership group at First Methodist would like the pastor to leave; the other half want her to stay. The majority of the people in the congregation haven't made up their minds and are not willing to get involved in the struggle. After each group sent a delegation to the district superintendent and failed to get him either to move the pastor or say she must stay (hierarchical decision), the congregation decided to try to make its own decision. They did this by bringing the people who wished to invest themselves in the decision-making process to the church on a Saturday. First, they had small groups identify specific, workable problems. Here the temptation was for the group that supported the pastor to give little credence to questions about the pastor's performance. The whole group then agreed on which problems needed to be addressed, after which small groups collaborated on suggestions for improvement of pastoral performance in specific areas. After agreeing on areas requiring improvement, the whole group decided on whether the pastor should stay and under what conditions. This process felt like an impossible nightmare at first but through persistence, caring, and support the group was actually able to "pull off" a collaborative decision about the pastor's tenure.

Negotiation is the decision-making strategy to use when collaboration fails. Here we assume that arriving at a mutually agreeable solution will not be possible, but that each group might get something it wants—though it will be only a part of what the group hopes for. Negotiation can only occur when there is something that can be divided or exchanged. It is not possible to bargain over a baby (as the story of Solomon and the mothers wisely noted). It is not possible to negotiate over binary (yes/no) decisions—for instance, shall we ordain gays and lesbians as priests? You have to be willing to trade decisions in one realm for decisions in another (OK, we'll vote to ordain gays, if you will agree to vote against the new prayer book). Negotiation doesn't work very well on theological issues, values, or issues of integrity. It is most awkward to trade a theological conviction about the virgin birth for a belief regarding Jonah's being swallowed by the big fish.

Negotiation is a back-up strategy to collaboration. If we can't arrive at a decision that will be satisfactory to almost everyone, then we can attempt to make trade-offs. This is most often done in churches over budget items.

But it can also be done over a pastor's tenure: "We will agree for you to stay only if you get further training in management." "We will agree for you to stay if you will call more." "Would you agree to leave if we paid you a year's salary in advance?"

Bargaining or negotiation gets less commitment than collaboration does. People go along, but feel somewhat coerced. And often, after the decision is made, the various sides spend a good deal of energy checking up on each other to make sure they hold up their end of the bargain.

When collaboration and negotiation fail, you can then move either to *voting* or *hierarchy*, depending on the polity and laws of your church. This is a last resort. Decisions so made leave many people very unhappy. It is better to make decisions in these ways than to let the conflict go on and on, but the costs are usually high.

Avoiding is another decision-making strategy. This is a decision not to decide and let circumstances decide for you. It is often not helpful except as a short-term, interim measure. Here are some circumstances in which avoiding might be appropriate:

- People are fragile and insecure.
- Another decision needs to be made first.
- The decision is not important.
- Differences are irreconcilable and confrontation would not resolve anything.

Bringing in outside help. Third parties are usually helpful in conflict management. Someone who is disinterested in the outcome can help the parties focus on their process, referee the fairness of the interaction, and provide an added assurance to everyone that they will be able to work through their differences. This "outside" party does not have to be outside the organization, just outside the conflict. It could be a trusted leader who has not chosen sides (and is not perceived by others to have chosen sides) or it could be a person in the community (perhaps a leader in a nearby church). Further, there are many resource persons provided by denominations, both volunteer and paid, who are available to serve in such situations, as well as professional consultants who work for themselves, seminaries, or such agencies as the Alban Institute.

What are the clues that would lead you to believe an outside consultant is called for?

- Clear differences have emerged and no progress seems to be made when the various groups get together.
- It feels as if people have lost control and the meetings are frightening.
- Parties are not speaking to one another.
- Conversations are characterized by attacking and blaming.
- Various people are trying to get the judicatory executive into their camp.
- Giving and participation have dropped off.

Helping all parties stay in the action. It is difficult to be in conflict with parties who have left the scene. Sometimes people just drop out; they stop attending or participating in any church functions. But other times they stay at home and participate by telephone. Other people then come to the meetings bearing the grievances of dissatisfied persons who are not present to convey their views accurately and responsibly. This kind of behavior is difficult and annoying to deal with. Anonymous or relayed communications stay at the point where they began. They do not change or develop as further information is presented. They are not conciliatory or yielding. Thus, every effort should be made to encourage all persons concerned to participate. Moreover, it should be agreed that only those who show up and participate in the meetings will make the decisions. Proxies should not be allowed and speaking for others certainly should be discouraged. One bishop I know insists that the participants at conflict meetings only speak for themselves. He strongly encourages them only to make "I think," "I believe," or "I know" statements rather than remarks such as "Some people have said," or "A lot of people are upset," or "I am only speaking for those who have spoken to me and are afraid to speak out."

Find out what is wanted by each side. Often people aren't clear about what they want, especially in the beginning of the difficulties. They can articulate their dissatisfaction and pain, but when it comes to describing the exact causes they find it difficult to say exactly what the causes are. Often, the causes will be bad "vibes" or poor relationships, but these "causes" seem not to be satisfactory "charges" to express the full pain that one is experiencing. What you have then is an uncomfortable person or group in search of reasons to buttress their dis-ease. These "reasons" often take the form of grievances—the pastor doesn't call enough, he wears jeans to church, and so on. Instead of dismissing these "causes" as inadequate, I have found it helpful to work with a group to help them articulate their pain and what they would like if things were going better. These expressions of "goals" or wishes are often issues or concerns that can be negotiated. A group articulating its wants and goals has a better chance of arriving at mutually satisfactory solutions than when it merely lists charges.

People often resist the suggestion that I help each group get clear about what it wants. They fear that I will make the other group stgronger and this will lead to more problems. Usually it does happen that the stronger groups are those that are clearer about what they want, but from this strength comes a greater ability to be more open, less secretive, and less manipulative.

Helping all the groups feel stronger. We know that the most violent groups in society are those that perceive themselves to be most powerless. You may have observed your own behavior as tending toward violence when you feel frustrated, ineffective, or are not having an impact on the other (for example, when you have spanked your children), or when you are most out of control. What we want to do in conflict management is to help all the groups improve their strength and self-image in order to diminish the likelihood of verbal or physical violence.

People who feel illegitimate, who perceive that other people think they are wrong, who are put down for their behavior, their cause, or their friends, are those who are most likely to feel justified in using covert, manipulative, and/or aggressive techniques to get what they want. Thus, helping each of the factions within the congregation feel legitimate, important, and worthwhile, as well as helping them clarify what they want, is most likely to disarm needless aggression and, hopefully, bring the groups into the open where both you and they can see what they are up to.

Problem definitions. I have found it helpful in almost every conflict situation to get all the involved groups to join together in an attempt to define clearly and agree on the problems on which they want to work. There are always more problems than can be dealt with at one time, and there is sometimes disagreement as to what the problems are. By asking the groups to come together and agree on problem definitions, we can take a first step toward moving the groups from a feeling of fight to a feeling of collaboration and problem solving.

Problem definitions usually take these forms: "Who is doing what," "Who is not doing what," and "Who feels what." Problem definitions always are specific, not general; descriptive, not put-downs; about the present or recent past, not the distant past; about possible, not impossible solutions; and written in such a way that there is high probability all parties will agree. Thus, "Reverend Jones' sermons do not have a clear outline," is a problem definition, but "Reverend Jones is a lousy preacher" is not (it does not describe specifically what is the matter with the sermon.)

Sometimes I ask groups of persons representing all the factions to write lists of problem definitions. Other times I ask the factions to work separately from one another. I use the former process when the groups can still "speak to each other"; I use the latter when they are too uptight to be in the same group. Once the lists are complete, I ask the total group (all groups together) to come to a collaborative agreement as to the three priority issues or problems to be worked on first.

The ties that bind. Every group that has had any history as a group at all has something that binds it together. This is usually called the "organizing principle" of that system. Quite often there are several organizing principles in one organization and these function as the glue that bonds the people together. These organizing principles are things like common goals, common history, common loyalties, and common values. When a group is experiencing internal conflict it tends to lose sight of its organizing principles. It tends to forget that there are or were important reasons to be together in the first place.

Identifying and reminding the group of these ties can balance the centrifugal forces (those trying to throw us apart) with the centripetal (those trying to pull us together). Asking the group what has bound them in the past, or why they are together now, or pointing out their common values and common hopes can be useful in affirming and strengthening the organization as it works through its conflict.

Dealing with feelings. Just as important as facts and logic are feelings (which are facts) and relationships. Emotions play a very large part in conflict and while it is useful to be logical and rational, it is not helpful to be so at the expense of feelings. Denied or unexpressed feelings stay with a person, cause later difficulty, or are displaced into other situations.

The best thing that can be done to help people deal with their feelings is to help them express them—to talk about them, not necessarily act them out. It is very useful to ask people to identify what they are feeling and to affirm those feelings. Telling people not to be angry or upset does not help. Asking them to share by describing what they are feeling and then indicating that you want to hear their feelings and that you can understand them will help the person feel supported, affirmed, and more in control than if their feelings need to be hidden or denied.

It is very important to understand that often the feelings that are being expressed are out of proportion to what is actually occurring in the organization. Sometimes people overstate their feelings because they are reliving or remembering traumatic experiences that happened to them in the past. For example, a person may have had a difficult problem with an authority figure many years before and now not only is experiencing the pain of the present difficulty but is also remembering and "re-feeling" what went on before. Moreover, it is not unusual for a person to feel strongly about something that is happening in the earliest stages of the experience and then have those feelings to abate somewhat—especially after they have been expressed. Therefore, hearing the feelings and then differentiating them from the specific issues can be a helpful step toward conflict resolution.

Providing structure. In the midst of conflict it is best to move in the direction of being more "law and order"-oriented and less laissez-faire in your problem-solving and conflict resolution processes. Therefore, I strongly recommend that you be clear about:

- Who is invited to what meetings
- When meetings begin and when they will end
- What the agenda will be at each meeting
- What all the steps in the resolution process will be
- When each person or group will be heard
- Who will make what decisions
- Who has the right to vote
- How any decision making will be conducted
- The rules of fair and open discussion

It is very helpful to outline the whole process at the beginning. Let people know how the information about the problem will be gathered, from whom it will be gathered, who will gather it, and how it will be presented. Also describe at the beginning what will happen after the information is gathered and reported. Be clear about who will get it and who will not. In the beginning let people know when they will have an opportunity to respond to what is going on and what has been said. And set a date by which you intend that the necessary decision will have been made.

Remember, structure will provide a sense of safety in which all can work with the least amount of threat. It will give people a sense of security that the process will be fair and open. Not communicating these processes early will leave people wondering if they will get a chance to have their say and have a fair chance to make an impact on the system. If they are insecure about being able to make such an impact openly, they will feel justified in using covert, manipulative, underhanded, or excessive behaviors just to try to get through to a system they may feel is "stacked" against them.

Communication. It is often the case that people have not been talking to each other, or they have been so cautious, vague, and less than candid that they communicate only partially with one another, or (in the worst situations) they have communicated invalid and inaccurate information. In these kinds of situations it will be very helpful to support the various parties in talking through their difficulties. Sometimes you will have to do a lot of encouraging to get the people to share their opinions and ideas. They will be afraid to tell the whole truth for fear that "it will make matters worse." Exactly the opposite is usually true (though not always; use your judgment in every case as to whether to encourage full and open sharing).

Another helpful idea for improving communication (especially between groups) is to have each group write their thoughts on large pieces of paper so that the others can read them. By putting them on paper the communicator feels that the message may have been received and is more likely to say it once and not repeat it over and over again. Further, those who have participated in writing it down will not feel the same level of need to get up and repeat what others have said.

I have also found it useful on occasion in large groups to have people speak to one another on a one-to-one basis. I ask each person to write down some things that they ought to be saying to others in the organization and then give them time to speak individually to five or six people in the room with whom they have not fully shared their concerns.

Most important with regard to communication is supporting, encouraging, assuring, and reassuring those who have not fully shared their opinions and feelings to do so. Sharing the feelings often diminishes the strong, negative emotions and gives the people who receive and hear the concerns the opportunity (though they won't always take it) to join with the others in some kind of a mutual problem-solving effort.

A FINAL WORD

The biggest problem to overcome in conflict management is the problem of fear. Our task as conflict managers is to help everyone feel strong, or at least stronger, so that they will be able to stay with the other persons with whom they are having difficulty. In conflict, people are not only afraid of the other (what might be done or what might not be done) but they are also afraid of themselves (Will I do something I might later regret?). Most of us are in conflict with other people in the church so rarely that we are very uncertain about the effect of our behavior on others, and are uncertain as to what kind of behavior is appropriate.

The effective conflict manager is one who can help everyone feel more confident that it is appropriate to share differences with others, and that once the differences are in the open we can search for ways to come to agreements that are going to have the greatest advantage possible for most people. People hold back their comments and resources when they are afraid. Our task is to help them share them.

NOTES

1. Anatol Rapaport, *Fights, Games, and Debates* (Ann Arbor: University of Michigan Press, 1974).
2. Rapoport, *Fights, Games, and Debates*, p. 9.
3. Rapoport, *Fights, Games, and Debates*, p. 10.
4. Alan C. Filley, *Interpersonal Conflict Resolution*, (Glenview, Ill.: Scott Foresman, 1975).

Originally published, in a different form, as A Lay Person's Guide to Conflict Management *(Bethesda: Alban, 1979).*

CHAPTER 3

Nine Common Sources
of Conflict in Congregations

Roy W. Pneuman

W hen I was a senior consultant for the Alban Institute, I sometimes worked with troubled churches. As I worked with church fights, I recognized some common patterns that I associate with troubled churches. Here I will first identify nine predictable sources of conflict, and for each suggest what "preventive maintenance" might be done, and discuss how a conflict that has become intensive can be de-escalated.

1. PEOPLE DISAGREE ABOUT VALUES AND BELIEFS

One major source of conflict I see in most troubled congregations arises from a difference in values and beliefs. Congregants disagree about what the church is and what it ought to be about. This disagreement means that the mission or vision of the church is unclear. As a result the church lacks clear goals or objectives. If goals have been articulated, we see little action in pursuit of them.

One way to prevent this kind of situation from happening is to work with the congregational membership to develop a mission statement. The process needs to produce broad ownership in the resulting statement. If the task is approached in a cooperative spirit, the mission statement can articulate these disparate values. In the process, the people can learn to appreciate and accept the goals of other portions of the membership. Once the mission statement is articulated, it is easy to develop goals that will express the mission and direction of the congregation.

This strategy can be attempted in a church where the conflict is at the problem-solving or disagreement levels, when the parties are still working together toward a mutually satisfying solution (see Speed Leas' theory on levels of conflict in chapter one of this book and in his excellent work *Moving Your Church through Conflict*[1]). If the conflict is at higher levels of intensity, where the win-lose dynamic prevails and people are intent on hurting, humiliating, or eliminating one another, none of the strategies that I'm going to describe will work without attention to lowering the tension level in the congregation. The prescription for these levels of conflict is to get outside help and get it quickly.

2. The Structure Is Unclear

A second source of conflict I often see in troubled churches is what I call *structural ambiguity*. These churches have no clear guidelines about the roles and responsibilities of clergy, staff, laity, or committees. The lack of clarity is a source of constant conflict: no one is sure who is to do what; therefore, people challenge anything anybody tries to do. This ambiguity can extend beyond formal structure and people's roles to the procedures and norms of the organization so that there is constant argument about the way things are done.

We see a similar situation in church organizations where some structures are formally articulated but people don't follow them. Because the persons or boards in charge of leading the congregation are either unwilling or unable to work within the formal structure, ambiguity prevails here, too.

Once again preventive maintainance is easy, but correcting the situation is often difficult. The church organization must be clear about its structure and about the power of the governing board to maintain and work within that structure. As churches grow larger they need structure more. However, even family-size churches (those with up to 50 members at worship each Sunday) need to have simple structures in place that are understood and respected.

3. The Pastor's Role and Responsibilities Are Conflictual

The role of clergy often provides a particular focal point for conflict. Clergy can help by working with the governing board to define the areas of responsibility the church will emphasize this year. Many denominations publish what is sometimes known as a pastoral activities index, which lists the many possible responsibilities of a pastor under such headings as worship, pastoral care, church education, mission interpretation, administration, and so forth. In my last pastorate I spent an evening every year with my new session to examine the 30-odd activities on the list. We agreed on approximately 10 to which I would give attention, and specified how much attention, on a scale from major emphasis to minor emphasis. The members of the session and I then agreed on who would take responsibility for the other activities. Whenever someone asked a member of the session, "How come Roy doesn't call on every member of the parish?" or "Why doesn't he lead the Sunday School meetings?" the session member could respond, "That's not what we've asked him to do this year. We can refer you to someone else." Later we expanded that process. We took several hours at the annual congregational meeting to invite the congregation's views on how their pastor should be spending his time. Once the leadership of the congregation and the members themselves had ownership of decisions about the pastor's role, there was little occasion for conflict over the role or performance of the pastor.

4. THE STRUCTURE NO LONGER FITS THE CONGREGATION'S SIZE

Changing size can be a source of trouble. A congregation that is growing or shrinking often finds itself operating in a way that is inappropriate for its present size. If a church is smaller than it used to be, it often tries to operate as it did in the past. A church that has shrunk in membership often has a huge committee structure. This puts tremendous strain on the leadership resources of the congregation to the point where people are burned out and volunteers are simply impossible to find. Here is a ready source of conflict.

In a church that is growing, a different pattern emerges. The myth of the "family" and the close relationships of the small church remains the dream. Yet, as a church grows, people experience close relationships in smaller groups within a large congregation. The pastor often expects to continue to minister personally with every member as in the past and that expectation is echoed by long-term members. Neither pastor nor parishioners recognize or accept the absolute impossibility of that kind of pastoral role in a larger church. Arlin Rothauge helpfully discusses the impact of congregational size on pastoral relationships in *Sizing Up a Congregation for New Member Ministry.*[2] In this classic piece, Rothauge describes four church sizes: the "family" church, which has up to 50 members in worship; the "pastoral" church, which has 50 to 150 members; the "program" church, with 150 to 350 members; and the "corporation" church, 350 and above. These different-sized congregations need different structures and have different styles of relationship.

Leaders of congregations changing size can study the effects of size on church dynamics, learning what shifts in structure and ways of relating will be needed. They can then help the members understand and accomplish the needed changes.

5. The Clergy and Parish Leadership Styles Don't Match

Troubled churches often seem to focus on the style of the clergy. There are various ways to describe the ways clergy lead and relate to parishioners, among them the Myers-Briggs Type Indicator and various leadership style instruments. Essentially these instruments measure two variables: how much attention the leader pays to task and how much attention to relationship. Whether a pastor is highly relational or not, some people in the congregation will not relate to that pastor's style. If a pastor is highly task oriented, some people will approve of the pastor's attention to task and some will disapprove. Clergy style often becomes the focal point in congregations where the departing pastor had either a highly relational style or a highly task-oriented style and the search committee reacted by trying to find someone just the opposite. In that case, the new pastor will satisfy the people who wanted a change, but those who appreciated the previous pastor's style will lament the absence of the qualities they appreciated in the past and do not find in the present. This reaction is particularly severe when the new leader follows a long pastorate. Alban Institute research has shown that a pastor who comes to a church after a long pastorate will almost always be an interim, either intentionally or unintentionally. Often one reason for this is that adequate grief work has not been carried out. Whether a congregation has grieved or not, the style of a long-term pastor has become so imprinted on the congregation that a change in style is likely to produce conflict.

A new pastor will do well to pay close attention to the leadership style of her or his predecessor. If the new pastor prefers to consult with lay leaders and to encourage their collaboration in leadership, he or she should determine whether the congregation's leadership is ready for that style. If the predecessor was more dominant and authoritarian in leadership style, then such an attempt to begin in the "consult" style is doomed to failure because the people are not trained to do what is being expected of them. A consult-style leader needs to work individually with each lay leader, gradually teaching and encouraging that person to take more and more responsibility and leadership, thus bringing about a new way of working together.

A new leader who prefers an authoritarian style will also need to determine the preferred style of the lay leaders. If they are accustomed to a high level of participation in the leadership of the congregation, dominating leadership will prove a disaster. The authoritarian leader needs to sit down with the lay leaders and negotiate just how the various groups and organizations of the church will operate. Indeed, he or she will need to soft-pedal the authoritarian approach and to channel it into parts of the organization where it will find acceptance.

6. The New Pastor Rushes into Changes

Many pastors arriving in a new church do not take the time and trouble necessary to get to know the congregation before making changes. I am not talking about sweeping changes, but about small changes such as introducing a new liturgical element, like the passing of the peace, into the worship service. Again and again I've heard people criticize their pastor primarily because that pastor instituted changes without apparent regard for the congregation's heritage and the feelings of its long-time members. Most of us want to change things so that they will be done in a way that we perceive is better. As tempting as it is to take the comments of a search committee or a few supporters as a mandate for that change, doing so is a serious mistake.

The best way I know to lay the groundwork for change is one I practiced in my last pastorate. During my first three months in that parish of approximately 150 members, I visited every home. During each visit I asked five or six questions that gave me the kind of information I needed to understand the heritage, the mission, the structure, the relationships, the leadership, and the procedures of that congregation. Some people advocate making changes rapidly and immediately. I could not disagree more wholeheartedly. Obviously those who offer such advice are not in the business of cleaning up the messes that kind of precipitous activity produces. Few changes cannot be attempted much more effectively after a pastor has come to know the people, has developed the necessary level of trust and understanding, and has involved them in the decisions to bring about the change.

7. COMMUNICATION LINES ARE BLOCKED

Every troubled church has communications problems and it's tempting to bundle all conflict under the catch-all heading of "poor communication." Often communication problems are more a *result* of conflict than a *cause* of conflict. When a conflict escalates, members of one faction tend to avoid speaking to the other faction. Information thus tends to be kept within each faction. As the conflict grows in intensity, each faction's perceptions and information become more and more distorted. In a troubled church, the information that is passed to the congregation from the clergy and the official board is often insufficient, and this lack of communication results in a backlash of anger from those who feel uninformed or misinformed. When the conflict reaches a level where clear factional lines are drawn and angry, and hurtful words and actions are occurring, the church needs to call in an outside professional. But a congregation can address its communication issues in ways that prevent the conflict from becoming so severe. For instance, churches can have open board meetings so that congregational members may come and be informed. One common mistake, however, is letting the open board meeting become a platform where dissident members can vent their spleens. I encourage every official board to adopt a clear set of guidelines for congregational participation in board meetings. For example, a period of 10 minutes at the beginning of the meeting could be set aside to hear expressions of congregational concern, none lasting more than two or three minutes.

Another way to enhance communication in the congregation is to offer congregational forums on potentially controversial issues. These can be structured in such a way that information is shared, opinions heard, and debate encouraged. Then when the board is called to vote on an issue, they will know that the congregation is informed and has had an opportunity to form and express opinions.

Printing complete board meeting minutes and offering them to the congregation is always appropriate. In most polities, the governing board is expected to have oversight over the functional and spiritual life of the congregation. Taking that responsibility seriously necessitates a clear and formal flow of information to the board from each organization in the congregation. When I ask official boards how they get regular information from all of the groups within the congregation, the number of blank stares boggles my mind. Of course, this recalls my previous comments about the importance of being clear about the church's structure and about the responsibilities and roles of each group in the church. If groups have clear, unambiguous responsibilities and goals, then it becomes a rather simple process to invite them to report on progress in whatever degree of formality the official board prefers.

Communication between the staff and the governing board is another potential problem area. Clear lines of communication between clergy and staff and lay leadership are critical for balanced leadership within the congregation. Clergy and staff members would do well to spend time exploring the "fit" between their leadership styles and those of their key lay leaders.

If there is a multiple staff, the way staff team members communicate among themselves is extremely important. I recommend a regular staff team-building event to keep staff communications open. Hold such an event at least annually and use an outside facilitator.

8. Church People Manage Conflict Poorly

The way people deal with conflict is a constant source of conflict in churches. Churches have developed a terrible set of norms for handling conflict. People seem to believe that conflict is evil and that it shouldn't happen in the church. As a result a norm develops which in effect says, "Even if conflict is there, we won't recognize it."

My first response to this is: Conflict is inevitable. Conflict is part of every relationship in life, and it is inherently neither good nor evil. Conflict creates the energy that makes change possible. Conflict becomes destructive only when we mismanage it. Well-managed conflict is usually not even recognized or labeled as conflict, yet we feel exhilarated when we manage our differences in such a way that each party comes away feeling good.

Second, when we deny conflict, we have forfeited the opportunity to deal with it constructively. When we deny conflict we have given up control over it and turned it over to someone else. More often than not, conflict that is denied or ignored does indeed become destructive; our worst fears about conflict are fulfilled.

The best prescription I know is educating people about conflict management before conflict becomes a problem. A good course in conflict management within the church is a good investment for church leadership, both lay and clergy.

Another destructive way we deal with conflict is what Edwin Friedman calls "triangling." Rather than going directly to the person with whom we have difficulty, we tend to go to a third person and play "Ain't It Awful." Then, of course, our misdirected communication burdens the third person with information he or she can do nothing about. It benefits no one. The person who is angry finds no release for his or her anger. The person who is being talked about has no recourse for dealing with the issues about which the criticizer is disturbed. The best advice I know for a person who is told something about another person is to say, "I think you need to go to 'A' and tell that person what you've told me. If you're reluctant to do that alone, I'll be glad to go with you as a third party." If every church member would abide by this procedure, we'd have a lot less destructive conflict in the church.

9. Disaffected Members Hold Back Participation and Pledges

In troubled churches we nearly always find a struggle over control of resources. As the conflict becomes more intense, people who are feeling powerless, excluded, and unheard find ways of surfacing their complaints. They may withdraw their attendance at worship and their financial resources and instead present letters and petitions. Control of resources usually becomes an issue because people feel ignored. Preventive maintenance includes balancing the leadership of the congregation so that each segment of the congregation, each person, feels ownership. People need to feel represented, to feel confident they can participate in and influence what's happening in the church. When the power in a congregation is unbalanced and people don't feel represented, those in the minority, feeling powerless, will make themselves heard in less helpful ways.

Too often troubled churches find themselves in a position in which the pastor and her or his followers are being challenged because the pastor has attempted to stack the lay leadership of the congregation with folks who support whatever the pastor is trying to lead the church to do and be. Unless the pastor is ministering to and listening to all segments of the congregation, sooner or later those who are not being heard will initiate a series of power plays that may ultimately result in the pastor's departure.

A FINAL WORD OF CAUTION AND ADVICE

Well, there's the list. It's quite a litany. There's nothing in the list above that can't be dealt with when the conflict is at the level of constructive disagreement. That's the appropriate time to intervene. Once any of these difficulties escalates to win-lose confrontation, it can be the dynamite that destroys healthy relationships within a congregation.

When I walk into a troubled congregation whose conflict is destructive I expect to see nearly all of the symptoms of church conflict that I have articulated above. I usually do see them.

The moral of the story is: Pay attention to what's happening in your congregation. If you notice any of the warning signs that I've indicated, do something to help alleviate the situation. If the situation is out of control, get help and don't wait too long.

Remember that conflict is the energy that vitalizes the church when it is used appropriately and confined within appropriate bounds. When this energy bursts out of control, it can destroy congregations and their leaders.

NOTES

1. Speed B. Leas, *Moving Your Congregation through Conflict* (Bethesda: Alban, 1985).

2. Rothauge, Arlin, *Sizing Up a Congregation for New Member Ministry* (New York: The Episcopal Church Center, 1986).

Originally published in Action Information *18, no. 2 (March/April 1992): pp. 1-5.*

CHAPTER 4

Conflict:
The Birthing of the New

Caroline A. Westerhoff

If we look around us, even without a great deal of scrutiny, we cannot help but notice that God's crazy pleasure seems to have been to make no two living things exactly alike: no two birds, no two leaves, no two anything. Rather than bland sameness, God does seem to favor the rich color and changing scene of intricately woven tapestries and lively conversation, albeit accented by the solid simplicity of plain cloth and the stark complexity of silence.

The nature of creation is differentness. I don't know why. At first blush it certainly doesn't seem very practical or very economical, although we must admit it is interesting. Uniformity and homogeneity would have been easier for God (and later, for us) to manage. But maybe good management isn't exactly what God is after. Or, more likely, perhaps we have perverted the meaning of the word *management* altogether.

We men and women are part of this creation of color and diversity. The God who lives in God's own company of the Trinity wanted company, and so that God created beings—us—in the divine image. And again, no one of us is exactly like any other who ever has been, is now, or ever will be. (We are not even consistent within our own selves from day to day or hour to hour!) We all are originals, and I am sure that you, like me, find this realization both exhilarating and sobering. It may be heady to see oneself as a precious work of art daringly and tenderly fashioned by the hands of the God who breaks the mold after the first and only casting, but we also must attend to at least three consequences that so obviously follow.

First, we are indispensable. No substitutions finally are possible. This notion is a humbling and fearsome one to me, not one of arrogant grandiosity. Aquinas defined humility as the patient pursuit of one's own excellence. We are called to be by God's grace who we already are, and if we and we alone can stand squarely on our little or large pieces of ground—wherever or whatever they turn out to be—then these spots will be empty if we are not there. They are holy ground, because God made them too, and ordained them so. Whatever is to occur there is important, and we are at least partially responsible for its happening. We are called to answer the divine invitation, to be there, to act, and no one can do it for us. It is true that, regardless of our presence or our absence, for now anyway, something will be different. There will be incompleteness, if only our own.

Second, every other person on this globe is indispensable also. Every other person must stand on her or his piece of holy ground if the present creation is to be whole. The inescapable word of God's plan is that each of our individual lives is precious and of utmost worth, and, paradoxically, we are bound tightly together by virtue of our very differentness. We would not be so joined if we were alike; then we would not need anyone but ourselves. We cannot escape our dependence on each other, try as we do, for our lives and fates are intricately tied up and entwined together: American worker with Nicaraguan peasant with Russian official with African baby with all children of the world's streets. We are moral peers. Indeed, we cannot even know who we truly are without others holding the mirror of their perceptions before us.

Third, we are obliged to call forth and to encourage the differences in our companions along the way. This is the essence of our being. This is the nature of leadership, properly understood. This is the work of the one who makes peace. To be who we are—creators in the image of the Creator—we must be actively engaged in the setting free of every other person to be who she or he is intended: someone different from who we are, someone who will see the world from another perspective, someone who will not agree with us. Anything short of such liberation is suppressive and destructive and ultimately death producing. (How presumptuous it is of us to think we might have a corner on the market of truth in the first place!)

We were created to be indispensable, dependent liberators. But such a self-concept will not be achieved easily by most of us. A radical turning around—repentance—will be required. Dependence, the keystone, is not a state we have been taught to acknowledge as healthy reality. We have too long been admonished to stand on our own, a posture finally and tragically impossible for us. Independence is antithetical to our nature, to God's intention. Our deep-seated notions of separateness must be seen as fantasy—deluding and dangerous dreams. To the degree we can see ourselves as connected to everyone and everything in the creation, we can be freed from the terrible burden of having to be right, of having to be adequate. We can fail—or rather we can admit failure, for fail we will. Our questions can become: How do you disagree with me? How do I disagree with you?

How is my understanding partial or erroneous? What do you know that I do not? Together we can tell the truth. A teacher of mine continually asserted, "If you accept everything I say without challenge, you will render me ineffective and will destroy my work." He was inviting his students to join him in a mutual quest for what is and for what can be.

CONFLICT AND CREATION

God creates the universe as a wonderful, giant puzzle with billions and billions of amazing and colorful interlocking pieces, of which you and I are but two. We can help fit these pieces into the breathtaking whole God intends if only we are willing to struggle, to find ways in which they can mesh with each other—not the same as becoming like each other. I think God expects us to be about this struggle. It is our part in the creative process.

The creative process always involves tension and conflict; ask any writer or painter or preacher or teacher or institutional leader. A knot forms in the pit of our being, often before the problem really has any discernable form. Anxiety, at times bordering on terror, swirls in the brain, as we confront the chaos we must allow and at the same time attempt to resolve lest it become disruptive to us and to others. (Another paradox: only after surrender can we begin to bring order.) Stage after stage of temporary resolution, glimpses of a resting place of calm and light, are followed by repeated plunges into the swirl until finally a solution emerges. A bit overdramatic? Perhaps, but only perhaps. Men and women alike know the agony and ecstasy of labor and birth, and we are aware they do not happen apart from some degree of tension and disruption. And we also know that the knot soon will present itself again, and we will be on that glorious ride one more time.

Conflict is not just inevitable, as we are prone to say wisely and with a sigh of resignation. Instead it is part of the divine plan, a gift. Disruption is integral to God's order. Conflict doesn't sometimes provide us with energy, insight, and new possibility as reluctant by-products; newness cannot come without conflict. It is not a price to be paid and endured, but a condition to be sought and welcomed and nurtured. In truth, however, we do not welcome conflict. We go out of our way to avoid it. We talk about *managing* it—that word again.

The root of *manage* is the Latin for "hand"—*manus*—and when I think of hands, I recall Michelangelo's great work from the ceiling of the Sistine Chapel, *The Creation of Adam*. God's hand is reaching toward Adam's, forefinger extended. In my imagination, a spark fairly sizzles in the space between them as God sets it all in motion for the very first time: "Be different, Adam. But you will not be alone in that differentness. There will be other different ones. Create with them." God's hand is open, although tensive. It is not shaking Adam into life but is energizing him by invitation. God is not actually touching Adam but is giving him room to respond and to experience his own life, his own vitality.

Perhaps Michelangelo's genius has provided us with needed fresh perspective. Hands—management—can be perceived as instruments either for controlling, checking, holding, taking, restraining, and even strangling or for guiding, pointing, stroking, kneading, giving away, letting go. To manage conflict then would be to allow it, not suppress it; to open our doors and windows to its fresh wind. Following this line of thought to its ultimate conclusion, violence and war becomes not conflict run amuck, conflict out of all bounds, but the final outcome of conflict quelled. They result when we will not allow the other to be different, when we deny our life-giving dependence on the different one with all our might and means.

RESISTANCE TO CONFLICT

If conflict, tension, is the given of creation and the creative process, why then do we resist it so? Why are we so fearful of it? First, precisely because it is the precursor of birth, and we do fear newness and change. We cling to the comfortable and the predictable because they are just that, comfortable and predictable, and we foolishly think we can control them. Remember the story of the people of Israel: even stagnation and slavery were preferable to the unknown of wilderness possibility. And, with them, we long to return to our Egyptian bondage—whatever that may be for us—because it is known and manageable, manageable in our perverted and sinful sense of the word.

But perhaps, even more sadly, we resist conflict because it is the result of our differentness. Most of us carry childhood memories of being different, and they are painful indeed. The young dancer from *A Chorus Line* says it for us all:

Now different is nice, but it sure isn't pretty; pretty is what it's about. I never met anyone who was different who couldn't figure that out.[1]

We have not been helped to prize our uniqueness; we render it a nega-tive. Somehow we believe that if we are different, we are not beautiful. But God's acts from creation to the cross declare to each one of us; "You are different; you are my beautiful child; you are worth everything to me."

And we are so afraid of God's other beautiful children, the other differ-ent ones who are strange and strangers to us. "We have so much in com-mon," or "We are so much alike," rolls off our lips with much more facility and relief than, "We are so different." But having everything in common is never true at the deepest levels of meaning and of relationship, even with those who are closest to us. We do not trust even these others, or perhaps more often and more honestly, we do not trust our ability to stand with them. We do not recognize the divine spark between us. And the consequence of this distrust and fear is that we find ourselves finally alienated and isolated from everyone else—as well as from the various and differing ones who occupy that mysterious territory within the boundaries of our own skins.

We were created to be unique, to be originals. We also were created to live in community. We were given the gift of each other. God saw that it was not good for the man to be alone, and made a woman, the symbol of all other companions, different from the man and at the same time fit company for him. We were created separately; the molds were broken. We also were created to complete each other—bones from our bones, flesh from our flesh. This is the paradox of our creation: we are single, yet united; solitary, yet communal; and conflict throws this paradox into high relief. We are afraid that if we dare enter the swirl of the wilderness into which our differences propel us, we will lose either our identities or our relationships. Or both. The issue becomes one of survival at the most essential and terrifying of levels. Either we could be merged into the image of someone else, no longer ourselves, or we finally could be left standing absolutely alone. Or both.

Resistance to conflict then is our need to control and to manage in our own way, to eat the forbidden fruit of the tree. It is our attempt to hide behind the flimsy covering of leaves, not daring to stand vulnerably before each other and before God. It is sin. And, as a result of it, we are expelled from the garden of richness and relationship, cast into an exile of isolated wandering and death.

How do we reenter this terrifying territory of conflict? First we must see our predicament for what it is, and we must see that all our fearful resistance finally and for all time has been overcome. What we could not possibly do under our own power has been made possible by the power of

God's grace. And then we just must will to enter. Courage has been defined as fear that has said its prayers: we generally act our ways into new belief and perception; we do not believe our ways into new action. Sometimes it will seem to be simply a matter of choosing how we will die—alone or in company.

We will soon recognize the ground around us; it is neither foreign nor untested. We have been there before, and we have heard stories of the journeys of others. From both we know that the feared loss of selfhood or of relationship does not have to take place. Our experience, rather, is that when we truly engage in the spirit of seeing what new thing can emerge from our differing positions, something generally does emerge. Admittedly, the new often is not exactly what we expected or even what we would have ordered; but come it does, and our relationship moves into areas of surprise and of greater depth.

Eight Guiding Principles

Once we do decide to venture in, there are eight principles that can guide our steps along the way:

First, we must allow gracious time in which to do the work. All time we have is pure gift, and we must receive and open the gift for it to be available to us. Our use of time becomes an expression of our thankfulness. To co-labor with others, to stay with the peeling away of layer after layer of disagreement, and then to gather together what we discover in the process cannot happen quickly or on an inflexible schedule. Premature definition of a problem all too often is our heresy. Further, to collaborate with others and to work with them in the richness of diversity and complexity, we must have been in their presence long enough and in deep enough ways to discover what our differences are. I am not suggesting that we must be on intimate terms; that is neither always possible nor desirable. But we must know each other, and that does take effort and time. There is mystery but there is no magic in birthing work.

Second, we must discern the rhythm of our work. A friend of mine asked, "Does this mean that we always have to be fighting? I could not bear it!" A dimension of time, but one important enough to merit its own mention, is rhythm—both in our individual lives and in corporate work. "For everything there is a season," the author of Ecclesiastes tells us. We cannot always be about struggle, and indeed the creative process includes the plateau of resolution and peace. Even God took the seventh day to rest, not as time out, but as an integral part of creating. Moreover, all of us do not have the same tolerance for conflict, whether by virtue of innate personality or of where we find ourselves in the other arenas of our lives at a given time. "It's time to quit"; "It's time to play"; "I will decide"—all can be appropriate declarations.

Third, clarity about task and purpose is essential. Too often neither is ever defined clearly, and to complicate matters further, what we say we intend frequently is not what we actually are doing! I find this particularly true within the church. Willingness to enter Auden's "Kingdom of Anxiety" requires some idea of why we are going there and of what we will be doing, so we can decide whether or not the trip is worth the risk and the effort. Questions that often stray into my head in the midst of dreary business go something like, "What does this have to do with our participation in God's reign of peace and justice?" and "Would Jesus care one bit about the outcome of this meeting?" I am quite sure they are not unique to my imagination.

Fourth, we need framework within which to labor. There must be bounds for the chaos of creation. They should provide a structure loose enough to allow for our weaving in and out of its members, sturdy enough to withstand the blowing winds of change and visible enough to provide a dependable and consistent environment in which we would be willing to engage in unsettling work. Of course I am talking about aids as seemingly simple and mundane as time boundaries, agendas, a suitably appointed space, and the understanding by all concerned that their purpose is not to bind, to confine, to cut off; but to allow, to guide, to shape.

Fifth, we must maintain a sense of perspective and of humor. We must not take ourselves too seriously; we are but pieces in the puzzle. To assume that the forward roll of the universe rests on our efforts is grandiose, desperate, and poor theology. Paradoxically, because God has taken us seriously, we can stand more easily and we can laugh. We are freed from the deafness and blindness of our arrogant need to control. We are freed to be present and available to our own selves and to each other. We are liberated to listen and to respond to the color of creation around us.

Sixth, we must each have special places to go for reflection and feeding. We have said that recollection of our experience, as well as that of others, assures us that conflict does lead to newness, not to destruction. And so we must have communities in which we carry on that essential work of reflection, places where we can tell our story and hear the stories of others who also travel along the way. These communities take a variety of forms: our families can be one, some are therapeutic in nature, and for many of us the church is that place where we tell and hear the overarching story upon which we bet our lives—a story of difference and conflict; a story of birth, death, and resurrection. It is that place where we regularly are fed with the power and presence of Christ in the eucharist so that we can continue to take up the struggle for peace and justice in the world. These various communities also serve as practice fields for us, places where we can intentionally work at striving together. Without the safety and encouragement they offer, how could we hope to engage in the larger and more frightening arenas of nation and globe?

Seventh, we need guides. We will find them in our communities. We also will find them in the unexpected encounter with the stranger along the road. We must seek guides for ourselves, and we also must be open to their appearing in the unlikeliest of times and places. Guides are those who extend God's hand of invitation to us. They are those who pass on the spark of creation, those who do not get in the way of our receiving it for ourselves. And we are guides, too: each of us is both Adam's descendant and God's sacrament.

Finally, we need times of solitude and silence. Only when we are most profoundly alone can we become aware of our deep center places. There we will encounter the Spirit that binds us all together. There we will discover the base of our oneness with each other. And only when we know we are one can we bear the strain of diversity—of birth. Only then will we have the courage—the grace—to enter that turbulence without which the balloonist tells us there can be no movement.

NOTE

1. Edward Kleban, "At the Ballet," song lyrics from *A Chorus Line* (New York: Columbia, 1975).

Originally published in Action Information *12, no. 3 (May/June 1986): pp. 1-5.*

CHAPTER 5

Creative Tension in Congregational Life: Beyond Homeostasis

George D. Parsons and Speed B. Leas

The seeds of decline are found in a congregation's successes. This axiom applies to individuals as well as to organizations. We pay a price to discover what will work in our lives. It is when we place ourselves (or are placed) outside of our zone of comfort that we learn and grow. New learning usually is accompanied initially by discomfort—recall learning to ride a bike, or to speak effectively in front of a group, or dealing with an angry friend. In this regard, we are by temperament all pioneers, curious about life and the world set before us and eager to find a way that works.

Yet, as our pioneering produces success, we are all likely to become homesteaders. The successful things we learned to do become our precious habits. The newly won ground becomes our home. Thus, as we successfully learned as children to handle combative parents by being the appeaser, or the rescuer, or the problem solver, or the fighter, we are likely to embrace that success and, as adults, rely more and more on that approach to conflict. Even in the face of declining rewards for using our time-worn approach, we will be tempted to refine those habits and depend on them. This is the tyranny of successful habits. As stress increases, we are likely to revert to those habits and to depend on them in a way that causes us to shun experimentation. The strengths born of our learning eventually become our excesses.

Many congregations are stuck in their successes. They can point to an earlier time of vitality and growth and to the efforts since to build on their success. They can often identify their strengths and the connection between those strengths and past success. But their successes led them to embrace organizational patterns and habits which no longer serve them well. They continue to exercise the same set of muscles while the rest of the body atrophies.

Congregations "succeed" because they are able to respond to need. They are able to connect their resources and competencies with the current needs of those inside the congregation and beyond. This organizational responsiveness (the pioneering dimension) helps congregations to adapt to a changing environment and to renew themselves. Most of the congregational decline we observe is the result of becoming adapted to the environment, finding a pattern that works, and staying with that pattern long past its usefulness.

What has worked well in the past now becomes the mandate for the future and we order our life accordingly. There is another danger, however: too much change. In reaction to our "stuckness," we may swing to the other extreme. A congregation we once visited had devoted major resources toward small group ministry one year, evangelism the next, Stephen Ministry the next. . . . Stretched thin by multiple program experimentation, lay leaders were exhausted and incoherent, and congregational direction was lost. When driven by trends or in their ongoing efforts to respond to a changing environment, congregations can lose their way, their identity, and their cohesiveness.

ORDER AND FREEDOM

Congregations, like human beings, live between the polarities of order and freedom. Between these two fundamental requirements lies the stage upon which the history of the people of God has been played out. The tension between order and freedom has birthed the great stories of the Bible and framed the historical struggles of the church. The tension is reflected in the order and structure established in the Torah and the later response of the prophets who both embraced the Torah and pointed to the need for change. The tension is reflected again in the post-exilic freedom symbolized in Ruth as a model of the new diversity within the people of God. The tension surfaced again when Jesus challenged the established rules about table fellowship and sought to enlarge the circle of acceptability. The Gospel of Matthew depicts Jesus as the embodiment of this very tension between order and freedom. Matthew's opening genealogy describes Jesus as both the son of David (connected to a history and a community) and the son of the new human being (a brand new person, free of the past). In this tension, the church continues to evolve and carry faith to the next generations.

When congregations live between order and freedom, not allowing the excesses of either to dominate, an atmosphere is created in which different voices and approaches are honored. The tension becomes something life-giving, creative, and renewing, as the "internal variety" encourages the benefits of both order and freedom.

I [Parsons] know of a married couple that embodies this tension. She is a financial planner, willing to delay short-term gain to build long-term security. He is a financial risk-taker for whom the enjoyment of life is a high priority. Over the course of their marriage, one perspective has dominated the other from time to time, and excesses at either end of this polarity have brought hardship. Sometimes his voice has prevailed, leading to the burden of debt. At other times her voice has prevailed in ways that diminished their here-and-now enjoyment of life. But mostly their two differing perspectives live in tension with each other. The tension, comfortable at times, certainly does not exist in some kind of a "balance." But their willingness to bring their perspectives into ongoing dialogue has made it possible for them to weather economic changes and the typical crises of married life.

Organizational theorists describe this same tension as a "loose-tight paradox." Business organizations, for example, need to be able to orchestrate stable production and marketing functions as they remain flexible enough to move with the ever-shifting economic climate and market variables. Family therapists also recognize this tension and describe it as a "integration-differentiation continuum."

Our very nature as humans calls us to be in relationships with others—a part of community—integrated into a human collective beyond ourselves. But our personal growth and maturity require that we differentiate ourselves from that community. At different points in our development, we may swing from one side of the polarity to the other, but it is in the tension between the two that we become fully human.

Since the forces of order and freedom are constantly in tension in congregation life, we would posit that healthy congregational systems will *create tension*—to maintain internal variety and stay flexible and open to renewal. Again, the healthy system moves along the continuum but is not stagnant and "balanced." A healthy congregation lives with certain kinds of contention created by the voices from both sides. We would argue that unless there are ongoing reasons for a congregational system to contend, unless there are opportunities to exercise these tensions, the congregation will lose its flexibility and experience decline. Without reasons to contend, congregations will experience either the excesses of order (which become overcontrol) or the excesses of freedom (which lead to chaos). One set of excesses is not preferred over the other. Either can kill a congregation.

CHAOS AND OVER-CONTROL

Congregational leaders can be unaware of the nature of their particular congregational system and not able to evaluate how effectively they are managing the order-freedom tensions. On the "order" side, poorly managed tension can lead to brittle or stuck congregations. On the "freedom" side, it can lead to disengaged or unconnected congregations. We have noticed that many congregations can exhibit some excesses on both sides at the same time; it is possible for a congregation to be rigid in some respects and chaotic or unconnected in others. But a congregation that is unaware of the excess (or loss of tension) may in fact treat the excess as the status quo or desired state.

As consultants, we find that much of the conflict we address is sparked by an effort to move a congregation out of an institutionalized excess. For example, we often enter a congregational system that has excessively concentrated authority in a small group of people. This group, though it may not be on the official church board, can informally control decisions and discourage participatory decision making. This excess of authority is often accepted as "the way things are." Pastors who survive in such a system learn to adjust to this power group. People unconsciously defer to the group and consult it about possible decisions. This excess becomes the status quo and the organization resists changing it. But often new members entering the system become tired or frustrated with this arrangement and act to challenge the concentrated authority. Conflict begins, in this case as an effort to regain a healthy tension by more broadly dispersing authority and widening participation in decision making. When congregations abandon the orderliness of good planning in favor of freedom, they will likely set a stage for ongoing conflicts focused on the setting of priorities.[1]

NOTE

1. Our book, *Understanding Your Congregation as a System* (Bethesda: Alban, 1993), features a Congregational Systems Inventory that we developed to measure

the approximate degree of tension in a number of areas in a congregation's life. A loss of tension indicated by very high or very low scores on the inventory will suggest needed change in the life of a congregation. The inventory has seven scales to measure appropriate tension. They assess the amount of planning in a congregation, the uses of authority, lay leadership, clergy leadership, the amount of attention paid to communication and decision making, the congregation's focus on the past or future, and the extent to which people work alone or in groups.

This article originally appeared in Congregations: The Alban Journal *20, no. 2 (March/April 1994): pp. 8-10.*

CHAPTER 6

Should I Leave?
A Letter from One Priest to Another

Warner White

Dear Harry,

I've been mulling over our phone conversation and I've decided to write you a letter. I want to speak as clearly, as systematically, and as theologically as I can to the question you're asking yourself, "Should I leave my parish? Should I be seeking a new rectorship?"

What struck me most was your telling the vestry at the time they called you to be rector, "I do not want ever to be the center of controversy the way Father Jones was, and if such a time arrives, then I will leave." I believe I understand your reasons. The parish was split apart over Father Jones. It appeared to you that very likely he should have left earlier, on his own, without being pressured into going. You vowed to yourself that you would never be the source of such discord, but today it seems that you are. You find yourself attacked by some parishioners and defended by others. You say to yourself, "Here it is. Just what I feared. I want no part of it. I will leave."

We talked well together the other day, you and I, because we trust each other, because, despite your newness in the priesthood, you are a mature man with much experience of human nature, and because you are also humble and want to "pick my brains," to learn from my years of experience. So here goes—let me tell you the principles of judgment I have come to and the experience that led me to them.

PRINCIPLE 1:
You are a symbol to your congregation

For your congregation you are not just Harry Woolman, you are *The Priest*,[1]
you are a walking image of something deep in the human soul. To understand
what is going on in a parish you must be very clear about the difference
between you, the rector, as a person and you as symbol-priest.

For example, from time to time I call on someone in the hospital who is
from out of town. Almost always they greet me with warmth and trust. I do
very simple things for them. I enquire about their health, we talk a little, I
say a prayer, I anoint them—the ordinary things that clergy do. Yet they
often react with immense gratitude—and admiration for me. I swell inside,
I have a sense of great power, of being bigger than life for them. I also have
a sense of unreality—I'm just me, what I've done is very ordinary, and yet
they are reacting as if it were very extraordinary.

What has happened? Is it me, Bill Hampton, they are reacting to? I
think not, for the reaction is far out of proportion to what I in my real
personhood have done. No. They are reacting to *The Priest*. What they are
seeing is not me, but me-as-symbol. I feel larger than life because this
person sees me as larger than life. To be a priest is to be singled out for
others as a symbol of divine power and caring. Priesthood is not a property
belonging to you or me; it is a clothing we put on for others.

After you have been in a parish for a while, and parishioners begin to
see your humanity as well as your priesthood, you can begin to notice how
at times they see other clergy differently from the way they see you. For
example, have you ever felt a twinge of jealousy at the fuss and bother, the
seeming excess of regard—the adoration almost—you perceive in laypersons as they prepare for the bishop's visitation? How do you react to the
admiration laypersons show for the visiting priest who has just said something you've been trying to tell them for years? I find myself thinking, "I
know him. He's just an ordinary guy like me. Why are they turning such
cartwheels? They don't do that for me!" They are seeing *The Priest*, where
you and I see just another of our peers.

From time to time parents laugh telling me of ways their children con-
fuse me with God or with Jesus. The children hear that I'm going on vacation and they ask their parents if there will be church, since "God is going
away."

We laugh. Isn't that just like children! But down deep it's also like
adults! The priest-symbol triggers deep hopes and fears and longings. Clothed

in priesthood, you and I evoke the longing for a loving parent, for the perfectly caring one who will make things all right. We evoke fears of wrath, of failing to please. We evoke deep hopes of being understood and valued by one who really matters.

PRINCIPLE 2:
The priest is always the center of controversy in a parish

In a parish the priest is not only a symbol, the priest is also a human being. The priest's mere humanity shows. The tension between these two factors, the priest as symbol and the priest as human being, is probably the most difficult problem for priests and parishes to live with. It means that at all times there are disappointed parishioners, parishioners who long deeply for *The Priest*, for the larger-than-life holy one of God who will rescue them, who will care for them—and what they find instead is Harry Woolman or Bill Hampton. Make no mistake—the large gap between *The Priest* and our personal reality is a serious scandal to many persons. They hope for much more than we are able to be for them, and their disappointment is deep.

Some parishioners never get over their disappointment. They become deeply angry at us and remain so. I have found such anger and disappointment very difficult to deal with. I have sometimes been tempted to leave a parish in order to escape it. But that's a mistake. Only if your judgment is that your weaknesses are so severe as to invalidate your sense of call, and only if your judgment is confirmed by observers who care for you, should this be a reason for leaving.

PRINCIPLE 3:
Pay attention to the character of the pastoral bond

When you and I accept a call to a parish, we and our parishioners commit ourselves to a pastoral relation. We exchange vows in a ceremony much like a wedding.

That step establishes the pastoral relation, but it is only the beginning. From that moment on what matters is the process of *bonding* between priest and parish. What matters is the way in which priest and parish become attached to one another in spirit, emotion, and behavioral pattern. The priest's pastoral task in the early years is the building and nurturing of that pastoral bond.

There are several elements in the pastoral bond—trust, caring, regard, power, centering, and the like. In a healthy process of bonding these elements go through various stages until the bond is established. I shall discuss three of them—regard, power, and centering.

The marriage encounter movement teaches that marriages go through three stages—illusion, disillusion, and realistic love. The illusion stage is the honeymoon stage, the stage in which the partners see each other through rosy glasses, in which the partners are on their best behavior. She is wonderful! Everything I ever dreamed of! She is the answer to all my longings. . . . Thus I see her more in terms of my own longings than in terms of her reality.

Then comes disillusion. I begin to see her humanity, and I am disappointed. This is a very painful stage, in which the partners can be very cruel. All too often they become so disillusioned they seek divorce. But if all goes well, the partners begin not only to see each other realistically, they begin to accept and respect each other as they are. When this happens the partners find great joy. Now she loves me for who I am! Now I love her for who she is! We love the real person, not the illusion. Now I am able to reveal myself to her without fear of losing her, and she is able to reveal herself to me.

I would expect the honeymoon between priest and parish to last a year or two, disillusionment to last three or four years, and realistic love to arrive thereafter. Any decision about leaving or staying must take into account the stage of the bonding process. Where are you in that process? What should be happening at the present time?

These stages can be applied to the bonding elements of regard and power.

PRINCIPLE 4:

A healthy bonding process goes through three stages of regard— adoration, disappointment, and respect

"Adoration" is a very powerful word to use for the regard shown a priest at the beginning of the pastoral relation. Perhaps it is too strong. I choose it, nevertheless, because it expresses the particular nature of the "rosy glasses" with which the priest is viewed in the honeymoon stage.

I heard a priest once describe how he was greeted in his new parish as "the messiah," "the one who was going to set all things right." "And the trouble was," the priest added, "I believed it! I thought I really was going to do all those things." He went on to describe his own disillusionment with himself, as well as the disillusionment of his parish when they discovered that he couldn't do everything they had hoped for.

"Adoration" suggests—accurately I believe—that the priest is viewed in divine terms. The priest-symbol is superhuman. When we start a new ministry that's where we begin. Larger-than-life hopes and longings are stirred up and are focused on us by parishioners. And we, too, are likely to have larger-than-life fantasies of what we will accomplish, of adoring crowds coming to hear us preach, of large numbers of converts through our ministry, of great social action programs being carried out, and the like. This is especially true early in our priesthood.

Then, of course, comes disappointment. We and our parishioners become painfully aware of our mere humanity. We and they are faced with the necessity of accepting a merely human rector instead of a messiah. If that task is successfully completed, and both priest and parish move on to the stage of respect, in which the priest respects himself or herself, and in which the parish respects the priest in that priest's humanity, a healthy bond of regard is established.

I do not believe that *The Priest* ever vanishes, however. Even when you and I are known as the human beings we are, we still remain, somehow, the image of *The Priest*. We still are walking symbols of God's care and love for his people. In a healthy pastoral bond the tension between humanity and *The Priest* is resolved, not by banishing *The Priest*, but by accepting the human being.

I have come to understand the meaning of clerical dress and of vestments in this fashion. These special forms of clothing are a concrete sign that the person who wears them is functioning as a symbol, even though he be merely Harry Woolman or Bill Hampton.

Notice that in the progression from adoration, through disappointment, to respect, there is also a progression in perception. At first parishioners know little about the rector as person, they see the rector mainly as priest-symbol. Later, if all goes well, they become able to perceive symbol and real person in harmony. They respect the person who plays the symbol and they accept that person's offering of the symbol to them.

I speculate that in many of those cases where parishioners become stuck in the stage of disillusion, the rector as real person is never perceived. Instead, the rector becomes the symbol of anti-Christ. "We thought she was the messiah, but she is just the opposite!" The rector becomes the symbol of betrayal at the most profound level.

Just as "adoration" may seem too strong a term for positive regard at the beginning of a new ministry, so "anti-Christ" may seem too strong a term for the negative aspect. And perhaps it is. Yet I have received letters from disillusioned parishioners couched in negative language so strong as to suggest depths of evil far beyond my limited capacities!

In these cases parishioners flip the superhuman coin. They flip from perceiving the rector as beneficently superhuman to seeing the rector as maleficently superhuman. They never perceive him or her as truly human at all.

PRINCIPLE 5:
A healthy bonding process goes through stages of power settlement

Group formation theory distinguishes three stages in power settlement— dependence, counterdependence, and interdependence. In a new group the members at first wait upon the designated leader to give direction. They depend upon the leader to get things going. Later they begin to see faults in the leader's performance and begin to rebel against the leader. Finally, group and leader develop patterns by which they depend upon each other.

These stages can be distinguished in the process of bonding between priest and parish. At first parishioners wait to see what direction the new rector will take. They look for clues to the new rector's intentions, and their general tendency is to cooperate. Later they begin to find fault, and finally they work out a pattern of decision making that is a balance of the forces within the parish.

PRINCIPLE 6:
The bonding agenda is set by the character
of the previous pastoral relations of the parish and of the priest

It is well known that parishes tend to call priests as rector in reaction to the character of the previous rector. If the previous rector focused on social action and neglected spiritual life, the parish is likely to look for the same in the new rector if they were happy with the previous rector and to look for the opposite if they were unhappy. This sets the parish's agenda with the new priest.

Similarly, the priest seeks to establish the same or different characteristics in the new pastoral relation in accordance with the priest's previous experience. This sets the priest's agenda with the new parish.

So two agendas set by past experience come together to form the details of what must be worked through in the bonding process. In my present parish I am very conscious that parishioners have been testing me on matters made important to them by their experience with my predecessor. I noticed that in the early months of our relationship they tended to interpret my actions in accordance with the character of my predecessor. I am also conscious that I have been looking for the likenesses and differences between this parish and my previous parish. *The bonding process is not complete until the past agendas have been dropped, and new agendas based on present realities have been adopted.*

You must ask yourself about the present controversy surrounding you, "What agenda is it? Is this controversy a leftover from my predecessor, or does it realistically concern me and this parish?"

PRINCIPLE 7:
Of special importance for the new rector are the bonding agendas of your predecessor's in-group and out-group

Your predecessor undoubtedly had an in-group, a group of people to whom he was especially close and who felt supported by him, persons whose needs he met in a way satisfying to them. He also had an out-group, people unhappy with him in various ways who felt distant from him. When a new rector arrives each group has a special agenda. The in-group hopes that they will have the same relationship with the new rector, and the out-group hopes for something better. The in-group will seek to continue the set patterns. The out-group will seek to change them.

Chances are that neither group will be completely satisfied. The new rector is a different person and will not satisfy the same needs as the previous rector, so some of the in-group will become unhappy. The new rector is likely to continue many of the same policies and practices as the previous rector, so some of the out-group will remain unhappy. The bonding process cannot be considered complete until the relations with these two groups have been worked out. Successful bonding requires that both groups perceive the new rector for the unique person that he or she is, and that they cease to perceive the new rector in terms of the previous rector.

PRINCIPLE 8:
The healthy pastoral bond is centered in Christ

One of the grievous ills of priesthood is the temptation to the cult of personality. A parishioner says of us, "What a great priest!" and we believe it. We must be clear that we are not *The Priest*; we are the *symbol* of *The Priest*. This means that both we and our parishioners must find our center in Christ.

In behavioral terms this means that the center of parish life must be worship, and in worship you and I as persons must be transparent—we must be symbol to the parish. Our persons must be subordinate to our office. Our vestments must signify more than our persons. Both we and parishioners must focus on Christ.

PRINCIPLE 9:
Listen to the heart of the parish

The heart of the parish is that group of parishioners who center in Christ by faithful worship, faithful giving, and faithful support and nurture of one another. They are the heart of the local body of Christ and he is at their center. They are bonded to one another in him and it is your bonding to them in him that is crucial. Listen to the heart. What do they tell you?

PRINCIPLE 10:
The parish must be viewed not only from the perspective of the pastoral bond, but also from a long-term perspective, in terms of parish history and norms

You spoke of how parishioners were in conflict about your predecessor when you arrived, and you spoke of the harm you saw them doing to each other. What you were observing were the established norms of the parish for dealing with conflict, and if they were harmful, then you were observing patterns that need to be changed. Any decision you make about staying or leaving must take into account its effect on parish history and norms. Will your staying or your leaving help those norms be what they ought to be?

PRINCIPLE 11:

You yourself have a history and a calling

You are yourself at a particular stage in your relation to God. God has brought you to where you are and God is calling you to take the next step, whatever that may be. Any decision about leaving or staying must take into account your own history and calling from God at this stage of your life.

ILLUSTRATING THE PRINCIPLES

Let me now illustrate these principles in two controversies from my own experience.

I have been the focus of two parish conflicts in the past eight years. In one case I decided that I must leave. In the other I decided that I must stay.

Last year was my sixth at St. Richard's. At the end of our annual meeting a parishioner moved that the vestry be charged to evaluate the rector's performance and to report back to the parish with a list of changes to be made or with the rector's intention to resign. The motion was amended to include the possibility that the vestry might give the rector high marks, and then it passed. I asked for a vote of confidence and received it. As you might imagine, the meeting was very upsetting to me and to a lot of people.

I discovered later that the parishioner who made the motion had gathered a group ahead of time in support of it. I was not surprised by his hostility. Nor was I surprised that there were others who were hostile. Some had personal disappointments. Others were angry about some of my policies. My attempts at understanding and reconciliation had not borne fruit.

The vestry, which included both supporters (the majority) and critics, spent many hours doing the evaluation, basing it on the criteria of the Book of Common Prayer and the canons. It was very painful for them and for me. They were able to agree unanimously, however, on a written evaluation which said, in summary, that I was adequately fulfilling my duties, and they appended a list of specific perceptions, favorable and unfavorable, of my performance. I responded in writing, and then we circulated the documents in the parish. That took care of the charge given us by the annual meeting, but it did not end the controversy. Vestry meetings were painful. I dreaded them, because at every meeting the critics harassed me about something. Two persons complained about me to the bishop. And during all of this I was filled with self-doubt. What had I done? How could I reconcile the complainers? And worst of all was the sinking feeling, the knowledge, that I couldn't do anything, that it was *me* they didn't like—me the way I am—and that my basic convictions were what led to the disagreements in policy.

During this time I received lots of support. I felt confident of the large majority of the parish. But I was aware of critics who had stopped coming to church and of critics who had withdrawn financial support. It was clear that we were going to run a large deficit.

At vestry meetings I kept trying to respond to the critics. I kept insisting that we work on reconciliation and that we strive for consensus within the vestry. But finally it became evident that the dissenters would have none of it. They were going to oppose not only me, but anything I proposed. This sort of strife was familiar in the parish. Some of the same people who were angry at me had circulated a petition seeking to get rid of my predecessor. Others had been angry at his predecessor. Power politics had been the parish norm.

I finally made two decisions: (1) I was going to stay; and (2) I was going to work with those who were willing to work with me, and not allow the dissenters to bring that to a halt. From that moment everything got better. Our energies were no longer consumed by attempts to reconcile the irreconcilable. Vestry meetings became easier. We began to get things done. One of the dissenters resigned. Another rotated off. And at the annual meeting the dissenters failed to win any seats on the vestry.

During all of this our Sunday worship and our sense of fellowship went well. There was no sign that dissent was growing; indeed, it was quite the opposite. We gained a few new families, and—most striking of all—our pledge canvass resulted in a marked increase in giving.

The controversy at St. Peter's was different. It erupted in my fourteenth year as rector as a result of one action I took—I fired the music director. I can still see in my mind's eye the coffee hour after the news got out. People stood around in isolated groups, and when I entered the room I felt cut off. Our music program had been a source of immense parish pride, even though it had also been the source of immense problems.

In this case a lot of my friends were angry at me. We called a parish meeting and decided two things: (1) the parishioners and I would hold a series of small group meetings to see if we could air out and work through things, and (2) we would get an outside consultant to help us find our way.

The small-group meetings were excruciating for me. They became garbage-dumping grounds. Parishioners heaped on me complaints that were years old and of which in many instances I had had no awareness. Vestry meetings were also painful. Friend was pitted against friend. Vestry members who had loved me and supported me were now my critics.

Parish life went on pretty much as usual in terms of attendance and giving and activities, but it hurt a lot. We were having a hard time with each other. The consultant talked with parish leaders individually and had a session or two with the vestry. Finally he advised me that in his judgment I had lost the confidence of the key parish leaders and should leave.

This had been my parish for many years. I had chosen to come to the neighborhood as a young man. I had been ordained from the parish. My wife had been born there and had grown up in the neighborhood. We had raised our children there. I felt a very strong sense of identity with the parish. I had never considered leaving. I wanted to stay, and I told the vestry so. We negotiated an agreement. We would have a parish vote of confidence and allow that vote to be our guide.

When the vote was taken I won by 60 percent to 40 percent. That night I decided to leave.

These two controversies came to different conclusions, and, I believe, the right ones.

First, the two controversies occurred at different stages in parish life. Here at St. Richard's we were still engaged in the bonding process and were at the disillusionment stage. At St. Peter's we had long before established the pastoral bond. Here we had been deciding whether or not to go on to the stage of mutual acceptance. There we were experiencing a trauma to the established bond. I had struck a violent blow to that bond, and the question was whether we could survive it.

Second, at St. Richard's there was a division between the heart of the parish and the dissenters. At St. Peter's everybody (with but few exceptions) was my supporter. Here it was the heart who wanted me to stay and persons outside the heart who wanted me to go. There it was the heart who said, "Bill, you've got to go."

Third, here the bonding process was proceeding successfully with the heart of the parish. I became aware as the controversy went on that I was in danger of abandoning that heart in order to appease a power-politicking group committed to other values and persons.

Fourth, St. Richard's has a history of divisions and of settling them by a power struggle—in short, a history of unhealthy conflict. St. Peter's had no such history; the conflict was carried out with a deep commitment by the leadership to the welfare of everybody involved. Here the dissenters sought to coerce others by withdrawal of support. There support continued throughout.

Fifth, I felt overwhelmed at St. Peter's. I remember those months as months of muteness. Whereas normally I am voluble, then I was subdued. Whereas normally I am filled with ups and downs of emotion, then I was overwhelmed with sadness. In contrast, my years here at St. Richard's have been years of blossoming. I have done a lot of writing and new thinking, and have received a tremendous response. A flood of creativity has broken forth from me.

As I see it now, my firing of St. Peter's music director was not only an attempt on my part to solve a deep parish problem, it was also (although I didn't realize it at the time) a blow for freedom, both for me and for the parish. As I see it now, I had become too identified with the parish and the parish with me. Rather than being two equal partners in a marriage, we were a merger of personalities. I was drowning and didn't know it. I needed to get free and didn't know it. Moreover, the parish needed to be free of me. They needed a rector with a strong sense of himself or herself as a person in his or her own right, a rector who would be more able to see them as they were and to confront them where they needed confronting.

Here at St. Richard's I am conscious of a different relation to the parish. I am conscious of a difference in me, of my ability to see them more objectively. Here I am much more conscious of the parish's needs as distinct from my own.

The crucial difference in the two cases is signified by the tactics of the critics and their relation to me. At St. Peter's the critics were my friends, they cared about me and sought to see to my welfare, even while they criticized. At St. Richard's the critics were foes, they withdrew support of both me and the parish, and engaged in power plays. They valued the Lord's

Table so little that they withdrew from it in an attempt at coercion. They had so little sense of bonding to the rest of the parish that they abandoned them as well. St. Peter's had healthy norms of conflict; St. Richard's had unhealthy ones. My staying would not have helped St. Peter's; my leaving did us both good. My leaving St. Richard's would have done harm, for it would have reinforced the unhealthy norms of conflict—it would have strengthened the tactics of withdrawal and coercion, and it would have undercut the tactics of support and consensus seeking.

There is much more to be said, of course. But perhaps the above will be of help.

Your brother in Christ,
Bill

NOTE

1. Readers from some traditions may find the term *The Priest* foreign. To catch the larger-than-life intent such readers should think of how Lutherans use the term *pastor* and some Protestants use the term *minister*. What is intended is the representational sense of the ordained ministry that evokes feelings and images of The Person of God, the one set apart to represent God's love and holiness for the people of God. *The Priest* may not be in his or her own person a holy man or woman, although some priests and ministers are; *The Priest* is the one who represents, signifies holiness. I suspect that this sign-aspect of ordained ministry is stronger in those traditions that emphasize the ordained minister's role as president of the sacraments, but I think it can hardly be absent from any tradition that ordains.

It is also important here to see that I am not making a theological claim. I am not saying that ordination causes such-and-such a change in the person. I am, instead, making an observation about what I observe actually happening. As a priest I find myself being experienced as *The Priest*, not just as a person. I find myself being experienced as larger-than-life. I also find myself sometimes being experienced as transparent; that is, as not being experienced as a distinctive person at all.

For many years I fought against being seen in a larger-than-life way and against being unseen as a person. I resisted wearing clericals. I asked to be called by my first name. I defensively emphasized joint ministry. But I found over and over again that many people still treated me differently from other persons, that many people wanted me to be different, that they wanted me to be something for them other than just myself. And for that it was necessary that I become transparent, that Warner White disappear into the background and *The Priest* come into the foreground. I finally made a decision: I would do it: I would be *The Priest* for them. And from then on wearing clericals was easy—it meant putting on my sign. It meant taking on the task of representing.

Originally published in Action Information *12, no. 1 (January/February 1986): pp. 14-19.*

PART TWO

Responding to Conflict

CHAPTER 7

The Illusion of Congregational "Happiness"

Gil Rendle

How and when did the American congregation become so sensitive about complaints? One very large congregation with more than adequate financial resources asked for help with a problem: a few influential members who contributed significantly to the financial support of the church were unhappy. They were not unhappy with what the senior minister was doing, but with the way in which he was doing it. Since most of the leaders were pleased with the senior minister, they were asking me how they could address the concerns of the complainers and make them happy. Another congregation, happy and healthy, asked me to work with its governing board to make some obviously needed changes in worship. But they were overwhelmed—and therefore felt powerless: every alternative they considered was matched with persons or groups who might be unhappy with the change. What to do? Often, congregational leaders want to "fix" their congregation, by which they mean correcting complaints and making it "perfect" for everyone. Instead, I suggest a healthier response: to work toward faithfulness rather than happiness. I advise them to go back to their mission statement or their understanding of their congregation's call to ministry and develop decisions that support such a position.

THE HAPPINESS TRAP

There are several built-in traps to using happiness as a criterion for decision making. The same is true for using complaints or their absence as a measuring stick of effectiveness. Perhaps the most damning trap is the constraining of the Spirit of God. This is the risk we run personally when we practice only the parts of a faith that we enjoy or appreciate. This risk was highlighted when an interviewer asked Huston Smith, widely known for his understanding and teaching of world religions, about his own spiritual practices. Smith said these included daily Christian prayer and Muslim prayer rituals, as well as Buddhist and Hindu disciplines.

Noting the eclectic pulling-together of so many faith traditions, the interviewer asked if Dr. Smith recommended such a potpourri of practices for others. The answer was a resounding no because people might then choose only parts of disciplines that seemed safe and comfortable. "If you only practice and attend to those things that you already appreciate and understand," said Dr. Smith, "you are assuming that you are already where you are supposed to be spiritually. You have left no room for growth and development that only comes from submitting yourself to a spiritual discipline that might in fact be meant to change you."

Such is the risk of congregational happiness as a criterion for decision making. If we assume that the only appropriate decisions for our faith community are those that will affirm what we already do and already appreciate, we have constrained the movement of the Spirit of God. That Spirit may want to call us to, and discipline us for, some greater maturity or purpose.

A second trap is that the happiness principle controls change by minimizing or eliminating it. Overattention to complaints is a predisposition to stability and status quo. This is often demonstrated by a congregation's personnel committee or any group given the task of evaluation. Many such groups are very unsure of how to proceed with an "evaluation" of such a nebulous process as "ministry" or "leadership." And so they ask what seems to be the obvious question: "Do we have any complaints?" If the answer is yes, then they move quickly to problem solving in order to eliminate the practices drawing complaints (that is, return the congregation to a stable status quo where happiness overrides complaints). If the answer is no, they often conclude quickly that their task is completed, and they report a favorable evaluation (that is, again supporting the status quo stability where nothing has changed sufficiently to create any discomfort that may have prompted a complaint.)

The third trap of trying to "fix" and continually perfect the congregation focuses the attention and energy of leadership internally and avoids or ignores any call to external ministry. Yet mounting research that defines vital congregations consistently stresses that they are clear about balancing their internal and external attention. They minister to current members and to potential members—as well as to those who will never be members.

In this moment when church leaders are looking about to understand which congregations will successfully navigate the waters of change from one paradigm to another, there is increasing awareness that ships that list out of balance in the rapid waters of change will be the first ones to sink.

A SYSTEMS PARADOX

In a seeming paradox, efforts to "fix" congregations actually bring an end to complaints less often than they create opportunities for additional and competing complaints. A reference to general-systems theory can be helpful in understanding this phenomenon. According to the theory, complex systems (like a person, or a corporation, or a congregation) have interconnected and interrelated parts. In the sciences, general-systems theory continues to provide evidence for the global interconnectedness of all living systems. This is true to such a high degree that, as the saying goes, "When a butterfly flaps its wings in the rain forest of South America, there will be tornadoes in Texas." In other words, any change in one part of an interdependent system will cause responding and rebalancing changes in other parts of the system.

In a highly interrelated and interconnected system, to "fix" one part is to throw the rest of the system into disequilibrium. Perhaps a helpful image is a mobile: a hanging work of art in which component pieces seem to be free-floating in space though the wires and braces keep them interconnected and interrelated. Changing or removing just one part of the mobile causes the rest of the system to swing through massive changes of position trying to accommodate the initial change ("fix"). So it is that an attempt to fix a complaint in the congregation often creates more complaints as the rest of the congregational system swings and shifts to accommodate the "fix."

Systemically it is normal that if a worship committee makes changes to quell complaints about the music, their response will spawn a scattering of additional complaints. The congregational system shifts to accommodate the newest change—meant to fix the problem. Similarly, when organizational rules about decision making are enforced to fix complaints that people are not following "proper procedure," new complaints will arise from others about red tape and the suppression of initiative. And when the pastor agrees with the governing board to focus her attention and time on the development of small groups because there are complaints about lack of fellowship, there will be a new outcropping of complaints about lack of pastoral visitation and availability.

CONGREGATIONAL REALITY

Rather than trying to solve problems and fix the causes of complaints, leaders in many congregations today are more appropriately trying to manage differences and make decisions based on the congregation's defined purpose or goals. The search for congregational "happiness" is not only difficult for leaders, but damaging to ministry. This reality is based in a fundamental cultural change characterizing congregations today.

We have changed from a culture of sameness to a culture of difference. There was a time not long ago when conformity and sameness were strong values to be followed. I often joke with people in continuing education events that when I was growing up as a United Methodist, if I left Philadelphia and traveled to Boston or Chicago, I could go to worship late on a Sunday morning and know exactly how late I was without looking at my watch. All I needed was to see where the congregation was in the worship liturgy and I would know the time. Worship services were fundamentally the same, as were the expectations of the people who worshiped in all of those churches.

This culture of sameness described not just the church. If you wanted to buy a refrigerator in the 1940s or 1950s, there may have been more than one manufacturer, but there were very few models of refrigerators from which to pick. The assumption was that everyone who needed a refrigerator needed the same kind. If you wanted a phone, you got one just like everyone else—big, black, and bulky, attached to the wall with a pretty substantial cord. Today if you want a refrigerator, salespeople are trained to "educate" you, not just about the tremendous array of models and features, but about yourself and your "refrigerator needs." Presumably, such knowledge will help you to pick just the right one in a culture of tremendous differences and choices. And what about phones? Recently in Atlanta I noticed that Radio Shack was having a sale on telephones and advertised "one hundred different models" from which to choose. I had trouble thinking of more than about a dozen kinds.

Ours is now a culture that honors diversity and differences. It is not a question of whether we should, or if it is good to do so. Sameness and difference form a polarity in which health and community are to be found somewhere in the tension between the two. Our present focus on differences and diversity is not the problem of ministry; it is simply the reality in which our congregations are living. Consider:

- More and more congregations report that between 40 and 60 percent of their new members do not come from the same denominational background as the congregation they are joining. They may not understand why the congregation works as it does because of its history or its practice. But they do come with some expectations of how they would like to see it work. These are real differences.
- Increasingly, congregations are receiving new members who not only have no denominational experience to match the history of their new church; they have no congregational experience at all. Not only don't they know how this congregation behaves and what it believes, they are not sure what to expect from *any* congregation. This group may not be sure what its new church home is prepared to offer, but they are sure they are seeking something and are willing to articulate it—for themselves, their children, or the kind of world in which they hope to live.
- Trends continue to show that more and more people are joining large churches (worship attendance of 250 or more on Sunday morning). Yet, ours has been a national history of small congregations (worship attendance of 150 or less on Sunday morning). Experience continues to say that the size of a congregation is the most critical variable in determining how it behaves, and that congregations of very different sizes behave in very different ways. This is especially true regarding communication, decision making, programs, leadership, and worship. Our congregations are increasingly a mixture of small-church expectations, large-church expectations, and non-church expectations, depending on the congregational experience that church members bring to their present congregation.

These are simply a few measures of the differences that are coming to characterize our congregations. There is an additional multitude of differences based on the variety of lifestyles and preferences of congregational members. Continually drawing the pictures of these differences and tracking their sources is critically helpful to our leaders as they seek to understand differences without taking them personally. However, pastors and church leaders are forever faced with the issue of how to satisfy multiple and often competing concerns or complaints.

ON NOT FIXING THE CHURCH

To approach this situation from the perspective of fixing the church or trying to make everyone happy is like stepping into a shower too quickly on a chilly morning. We instinctively reach for the hot water and turn it up hoping to fix the problem, but end up unbalancing the system. The shower then becomes too hot because we have overattended to the hot water. We then have to reach for the cold, often in the process further unbalancing the system and requiring that we play with the faucets a third or fourth time. The more you play with the faucets, trying to "fix" the water temperature, the longer the system stays in disequilibrium.

So, too, trying to satisfy each and every demand in the congregation (or the judicatory) does not lead to improvement, or even satisfaction of the complaints. It simply keeps the system out of balance and in a reactive mode as various expectations compete.

A training event with clergy and laity who were preparing to try to help congregations go through transformational change explored this systems paradox. One of the group members later sent me a computer graphic of a bathroom shower with a heading that said, "Keep your hands off the faucets." That may not be a bad maxim for congregational leaders who are experiencing complaints. We need to encourage leaders to stop trying to adjust the water to make it comfortable for everyone, and to stop trying to fix every complaint.

Instead, congregational leaders need to begin learning more about their congregations rather than trying to fix them. Obviously, ignoring complaints may be even more dangerous than trying to fix them. Differences and dissatisfactions that go without any response lead to divisions and mistrust. Congregational leaders, both clergy and lay, need to let their members know that their concerns and complaints have been heard. But then, congregational ministry, especially in a changing environment, is better served if leaders expend their energy trying to understand why their congregational systems react or respond as they do rather than trying to fix them. We clearly need to "unhook the system" from our earlier congregational expectations of sameness, and from the need to think that harmony and community depend upon everyone being "happy."

UNHOOKING THE SYSTEM

I remember a particularly frustrating "game" from my childhood. My sister would decide that I was in a bad mood and needed to smile, or simply that I needed to be irritated. She would begin to mimic everything I said and did as a way of getting me either to laugh or to scream. If I whistled, she whistled. If I looked out the window, she looked out the window. If I said "Stop it," she said "Stop it." If I yelled, "Mom!" she yelled "Mom!" What was truly frustrating about this "game" was that there was no way to end it. Whatever I did to bring the game to an end was mimicked and became the next step in the game itself.

A congregation today is a social institution of increasing differences and complexity. Each time leadership tries to satisfy a complaint in this complex reality, it does not return the congregation to happiness or satisfaction (the end of the game). Instead, "fixing" a complaint, in interrelated and interconnected systems such as congregations, becomes the next stop in the game of differences, and spawns the next complaint from some other part of the system.

Congregational leaders, clergy and laity alike, are seeking ways to end the complaint game. They are learning to make decisions based on their understanding of the congregation's call to ministry or its core purpose, rather than according to an individual's or group's preferences. This often means managing differences in the congregation rather than harmonizing them, or managing differences in order to preserve them rather than negotiating differences into common agreement. It means "unhooking" the congregational system from the "we need to fix it" complaint game.

CHANGING THE QUESTIONS LEADERS MUST ANSWER

One of the fundamental ways of unhooking the system from the "fix-it" syndrome is to be intentional about the questions that leaders are asked to address.

I worked once with an expanded personnel committee in a congregation that was experimenting with a new and potentially exciting form of ministry involving multiple staff. After several years they had concluded that the idea was still good but that it just wasn't working. They had recently experienced their second round of substantial complaints from congregation members.

When I asked the committee to explain the mission or purpose of their new experiment in ministry, I received multiple and contradictory interpretations from people around the room. When I asked them to explain their purpose as a personnel committee, again they offered multiple explanations. When I asked what they did as a committee to help implement the new experiment, the chairperson responded by saying that they really didn't have a clear role. Rather, they just reacted to problems that staff encountered. This group of leaders was constantly facing *problem questions*:

- Who wants what?
- How do we satisfy . . . [a person or a group]?
- What should we do about . . . [a problem or a complaint]?

Leaders and committees benefit greatly in escaping the "fix-it" game by reframing questions they seek to answer. The goal is to minimize the problem questions and refocus on *purpose and identity questions*:

- Who are we and who are we called to be?
- What are we called to do in this chapter of our history as a congregation?
- What are the goals and/or objectives that we set out to accomplish in our ministry?
- What are the appropriate strategies for our ministry, and how will we measure its attainment?

Staying focused on purposeful questions instead of problem questions helps remind leaders that change is expected in their congregation and their ministry. They are then more easily reminded that changes in a congregational system are often accompanied by complaints. They can begin to explore those complaints or discomforts as possible evidence of their goals in ministry rather than as barriers. It is quite a different perspective for leaders to discuss if they have been receiving complaints "appropriate to" defined goals of ministry, than to discuss trying to keep everyone satisfied as they try to initiate changes.

DEALING WITH WITHDRAWAL

Making the shift from a fix-it posture to purposeful leadership is often a change in the congregational system itself and will provoke reactions in the congregation as the system tries to rebalance and find equilibrium. As in withdrawal from caffeine, there will be headaches. The congregational system will initially become more reactive and complaining, not less so. According to family systems theory, when a family system seeks to change for the better through therapy or some other intervention, the family initially gets worse (becomes more reactive) before it gets better. It is easy to see this in the frustrating game of mimic from my childhood. When I finally figured out that the only way to stop my sister from irritatingly copying everything that I said and did was to stop saying and doing things, it initially intensified the game. My sister would then begin to exaggerate her mimic of any movement, gesture, or even breathing of mine as a way of prompting some kind of reaction reintroducing the game.

Similarly, when the pastor and other leaders stop responding to complaints by trying to fix them and begin trying to understand and interpret them, the congregation (especially those with the complaints) will intensify energy and excitement around the complaints. Withdrawal from the complaint game can be uncomfortable.

At such a time, it is more helpful if leaders take a nonreactive and "self-differentiating" position. This is a family systems theory response Edwin Friedman introduced for congregational leadership. Leaders need to maintain three significant postures in their effort to be nonreactive and self-differentiated:

1. Stay connected
2. Take a clear and reasoned position
3. Resist sabotage

Stay Connected

Staying connected depends on communication. Leaders must listen to individuals and groups to understand how the congregation is reacting. And they need to talk with individuals and groups about what is taking place and its purpose. To become disconnected—to ignore or dismiss complaints or discomfort in the congregation—is both foolish and inappropriate. People need to be heard and responded to.

Staying connected begins with listening. People need to be taken seriously as they respond to changes within their congregation. Author Steven Covey identifies listening as the most important and powerful communication tool in his principle, "Seek first to understand, then to be understood."[1] When we try to help someone understand the need for a change in the worship service, or in the use of the pastor's time, or in the allocation of money, we too often begin by talking instead of listening. Our cultural training is such that even when we do listen, it tends to be limited to searching for the information needed to shape our next response.

A major part of staying connected is listening to understand the congregation's issues (not to fix its complaints). Leaders can sit down in conversation with individuals who seem to voice concerns on behalf of others. They can invite concerned subgroups to meet with a few congregational leaders or with the governing board. They can convene systematic listening groups at times of significant change or challenge. In any case, listening is most successful when people are assured that they are heard. Whether as a conclusion to an informal conversation or as a written report to the whole congregation listing responses from congregation-wide listening groups, there needs to be a way to say to people, "This is what we heard you say about your hopes and concerns." People will correct any inaccuracies.

The second part of staying connected is talking. Leaders need to continue to talk and inform members of what they are doing, and why. If there is a vision of ministry driving leaders' actions, people need to be told repeatedly about it and how the present actions, decisions, programs, or priorities are connected to that vision. It is a matter of extraverting. In the familiar preferences of the Myers-Briggs Type Indicator, persons (and congregations) who introvert do all of the necessary thinking and planning internally and then announce conclusions. Congregations "introvert" when they do all of their thinking and planning in committee meetings and announce only the decisions to the congregation. Decisions and conclusions offered only in an introverted fashion may be absolutely appropriate and correct, but they are disconnected from the vision and the process that led the congregation to a particular change or priority. An essential tool for leaders in staying connected is to extravert. If there is a rule of thumb here it might be that leaders need always to extravert their process and the content of their process as often as they can.

Take a Clear and Reasoned Position

Listening to people or groups as they share their concerns or complaints is not a contract to agree with them. People have a right to be heard, but they do not hold a mandate to be accommodated. Yet many congregational leaders are often hard-pressed to point to reasons or criteria that guide their decision making. Without this reference, leaders appear to others as if they are simply following their own preferences and choosing against the preferences of the complainers. This is the basis of many congregational arguments ending with the conclusion that if "we don't like the way that our pastor/board decides this issue, then we'll call/elect new people next time."

Leaders must address the purpose questions in advance: Who are we? To what have we been called? What are our goals, objectives, strategies? When leaders have clarity and consensus around these purpose questions, it is much easier to take a clear and reasoned position in response to congregational complaints and concerns. Leaders' clarity about purpose questions provides the necessary "why's" to explain decisions to the congregation. "Yes, the pastor is visiting the shut-ins less frequently this year and the reason is . . ." "Yes, there is a significant increase in the budget for music this year instead of redecorating the adult fellowship room because we are intentional about our goal of . . ."

Resist Sabotage

Sabotage is a rather strong word. It does, however, recognize the resistance and the continued reactivity that occur when people or groups in the congregation do not get the answer they wanted to their complaints. People in the community need the safety of time and space to work through internal personal and spiritual transitions that will come with any significant changes. After leaders take a clear and reasoned position, time and space are necessary for people to react and respond. Leaders should not participate in the reactivity; they need to hold their course during this period. Resisting "sabotage" does not mean "fighting back" in order that leaders "win" and members "lose." It has more to do with leaders:

- working to *understand, rather than evaluating* and defeating the responses of disequilibrium they are receiving

- completing communication with all interested and involved people to make sure everyone has the same information at the same time
- depersonalizing reactions so they are seen as expressions of discomfort or change rather than as expressions of hostility or evaluations of poor leadership directed at decision makers
- being willing to be vulnerable with critics without giving in to coercion to change a decision
- drawing upon the humor and play that are healthy and health-giving in any relationship, and that allow us to smile and joke with each other even at difficult times
- honoring the chaos that accompanies any time of great change

"Unhooking" congregational systems from our learned behavior of trying to please everyone is a shift that will create reactions and complaints of its own. It requires congregational leaders to acquire new skills and commitments. It requires from leaders an understanding of the congregational system and a committed willingness to focus on the ministry's vision and purpose. Such a leadership shift may be an essential key to a viable future in congregations trying to stay connected and relevant to a changing world.

NOTE

1. Steven Covey, *The Seven Habits of Highly Effective People* (New York: Simon & Schuster, 1989), p. 235.

Originally published in two parts in Congregations: The Alban Journal *23, no. 3 (May/June 1997): pp. 15-17 and no. 4 (July/August 1997): pp. 14-17.*

CHAPTER 8

When Criticism Comes: Understanding and Working through Our Defensiveness

James A. Sparks

Criticism won't kill us but, as we all know from personal experience, it sure hurts. Everyone who has served the public in any way has been and will be subject to criticism. Complaints arise naturally from the expectations of a society driven by a consumer mentality. So when laity and clergy encounter complaints within the context of ministry, it should be no great surprise. What does surprise leaders of congregations is an emerging lack of civility behind some of the complaints, sometimes even emotional abuse. If you've been stung by this kind of personal attack, you know that terrible feeling of loneliness and the difficulty of coping with even legitimate criticism.

At least three leading authorities on clergy issues have begun to address the problem of mean-spirited behavior in congregations—Wayne Oates in *The Care of Troublesome People*, Peter Steinke in *How Your Church Family Works*, and Lloyd Rediger in his article "Managing the Clergy Killer Phenomenon."[1] Our pain to which these experts speak makes a discussion of defensiveness—whether in reaction to verbal abuse or to the ordinary garden-variety ministry complaints—vitally important for laity and clergy. If we're unaware or unaccepting of our defensiveness, we're likely to view all anger and every criticism as a personal assault. This can block off useful feedback and prevent us from ministering to the needs of people with valid concerns. Feeling defensive, we may villainize the critic while justifying our actions or omissions to ourselves and others.

The Roman Catholic contemplative writer Henri Nouwen describes his own defensive reactions in this way:

> I hardly remember what it was, but a small critical remark and a few irritations during my work in the bakery were enough to tumble

me head over heels into a deep, morose mood. Many hostile feelings were triggered and in a long sequence of morbid associations,
I felt worse and worse about myself, my past, my work, and all the
people who came to mind. But happily I saw myself tumbling and
was amazed how little was needed to lose my peace of mind and
to pull my whole world out of perspective. Oh, how vulnerable I
am![2]

Nouwen names the two most common emotional and spiritual injuries
resulting from being criticized—interrupted peace of mind and temporary
loss of perspective. Even when the messenger makes careful efforts to
soften the complaint with descriptors such as "constructive," "valid," or
"helpful," such words often don't allay our negative attitudes about the
message or change our defensive reactions toward the messenger. What
Nouwen calls "a deep, morose mood" describes a jumble of feelings, physical symptoms, and behaviors designed to fend off the "attacker." Initially
this may mean fighting back or getting even with the complainer. Afterwards, defensiveness easily evolves into "a long sequence of morbid associations" as we internalize what's happened.

To understand what happens when we "get defensive" and to find a
different way of dealing with these reactions, I invite you to think of a
recent confrontation when someone was angry with you or critical of you.
Choose an incident that tugged at your defensive feelings and worried you
afterward. With that image in mind, note on a piece of paper the following:

1. When the person came to you . . .
   a. How did you feel?
   b. How did you react physically (sweaty hands, etc.)?
   c. What did you say or do?

2. Afterwards as you thought about it in off hours . . .
   a. How did you feel?
   b. How did you react physically?

3. Now as you look back . . .
   a. How do you feel about what happened?
   b. Has there been closure to the incident?

DEFENSIVENESS: THE TRAUMA PHASE

Now, let's see how your feelings and physical reactions compare with the reports of others who have participated in this exercise. For example, I once asked 120 Milwaukee paramedics to compare their initial physical distresses in response to angry or even abusive criticism with what they hear from victims in medical emergencies. The paramedics responded as I have heard other medical workers respond over the years. Their distresses included cold sweats, rapid pulse, nausea, tingling and numbness, dry mouth, shaky voice, dizziness, and trembling. They reported feelings of anger, hurt, betrayal, surprise, embarrassment, shock, as well as a perception of being personally attacked. When I asked what medical emergencies gave rise to similar physical symptoms, they named heart attacks, acute anxiety, and drug overdose. The physical impact of criticism expressed in defensive reactions can't be overstated.

The term *trauma* I think aptly describes this state of defensiveness. For Nouwen the criticism was "enough to tumble me head over heels into a deep, morose mood." As in other kinds of trauma, we experience a kind of mental numbness while the rest of the body prepares to defend or fight with a sudden rush of adrenaline.

A common defensive reaction is to start talking and lapse into what I call "motor-mouth overdrive." If we can talk or argue our way through the critic's anger, we reason, then everything will be fine. But we may end up in a shouting match, with one party or the other feeling victimized.

In a confrontational situation there's often very little we can do to stop the action or escape our internal defensive feelings. The confrontation takes on a life of its own until it stops. This doesn't mean we're helpless or powerless. Contrary to ingrained survival instincts to try either to defend ourselves or to change the critic's mind, we can take limited but effective steps to deal with the trauma experienced during a confrontation. Here are some suggestions that may help:

1. *Apply the "look straight, don't brake" principle.* Not long ago, I was driving the interstate between Madison and Milwaukee, taking it at about 68 mph since there wasn't much traffic. As the sun poked through the horizon, illuminating trees and bushes covered with hoary frost, I approached the crest of a long grade. When I started my descent down the other side I saw a jackknifed 18-wheel truck at the bottom of the grade

along with police cars, fire trucks, and other cars in the median. I realized that the frost had coated the road with ice crystals. Instinctively I went for the brake, but backed off when something in my head said, "Look straight, don't brake." I gripped the wheel, kept my foot off the brake, and steered through the mess without incident.

When you've been surprised with a potentially dangerous situation like the one I just described, you go into shock and, without thinking, you do what it takes to save your skin. In a confrontation, that defending instinct is to justify yourself compulsively. "Look straight, don't brake" means carving out a new mental path for dealing with either an icy road or a critical confrontation. It's a conscious effort to stop justifying. Say to yourself, "Stay quiet, stay quiet, stay quiet."

2. *When you hear complaint, think INFORMATION.* This is another helpful form of self-talk. Viewing criticism as information can help us deal more objectively with the complaint as a problem to be solved or an issue to be clarified. In other words, the criticism may be right on track despite how different our perception is from the critic's. It's important to listen for facts and specifics, even when reported angrily. Something we've done or not done has upset the critic enough to tell us about it. On the other hand, if the critic comes at us distraught, short on specifics, perhaps abusive, that behavior carries important information. It's pointless to join the battle. What that person needs is to let off steam. Take a deep breath and say to yourself: "This is information. This is information. This is information."

Defensiveness: The Brooding Phase

Now refer again to your notes about what happened after the criticism. Did you worry excessively? Did you float in and out of alternating periods of anger and resentment? If you did, you're not alone. This is what I call the brooding stage of defensiveness. You know you're in it if you experience any of the following three reactions:

1. *Self-blame.* Here is where we turn the critic's complaint inward and add our own critical imaginings to send us into a downward spiral of negative and esteem-destroying thoughts. Here is where we are likely to believe the critic's worst assessments. Even if the criticism alleges a relatively small error or omission, we are likely to beat ourselves severely for having

made the mistake. "How could I have been so careless and inattentive?" "How could I have been insensitive [meaning 'stupid'] enough to have made that comment?" You know how it goes.

2. *Obsessing.* When we are feeling hurt and down, a mental tape replays the confrontation over and over again. Even while we're trying to relax at home, sleep during the night, or return to work the next day, the mental tape intrudes.

3. *Fantasizing.* One of the most frequently reported fantasies of people hurt by criticism they feel is unfair or undeserved is the wish "to get even." They have felt so injured, they imagine ways that injury or illness (even death) might be visited on the one who has injured them. The next most reported fantasy has to do with changing jobs to escape criticism, to start over in the hope that the next call or assignment will be different. This fantasy thrives on the belief that it's possible to avoid criticism the next time. A third fantasy, common in people-intensive vocations like ministry and nursing, is that if you work hard enough and sacrifice enough, people will like you and not intentionally hurt you—that is, they will not criticize you unjustly or hurtfully.

Understanding and accepting our brooding defensive feelings is important for our emotional well being. But like any other depressive or down mood, it's difficult to stand back and reflect objectively. I have found certain tactics helpful, however, in working through this phase.

1. *When you feel sad or angry, acknowledge out loud to yourself how upset you feel.* Instead of numbing your feelings with food, alcohol, or medications, affirm that your feelings are normal under the circumstances. In other words, you are entitled to feel lousy. There is no need to heap on additional negatives.

2. *Own the resentment you may feel toward the critic or perpetrator of the pain.* Your resentful feelings will be there, oozing into consciousness even as you may try to dampen them with prayer or intentional spiritual reflection. Nevertheless, just naming the negative mental activity validates it as part of the recovery process.

3. *Interrupt your brooding with physical activity or pleasant mental images.* The late Wayne Oates, a long-time clergy watcher, advocated taking "five-minute vacations" to reduce stress. Such interruptions can include a short walk, or having a pleasant lunch with a colleague, or going off to some favorite vacation spot in a five-minute daydream.

4. *Tell it to a friend.* When we have felt injured by criticism—especially unfair criticism—some will choose to endure it without telling anyone about it. Others choose to tell everyone who'll listen, particularly their spouses or others with whom they live. Putting spouse, family, or members of your religious community into the counselor role places undue burden on these important relationships. Let people who live with or near you know that you are feeling distracted and that you may need some quiet time. Then call a friend. Talk over the phone or make a date for breakfast or lunch. Choose a friend who will listen and not give advice. If you need more than this, you may be wise to seek a professional counselor.

DEFENSIVENESS: THE RECOVERY PHASE

Recovery begins when we stop obsessing about our pain and looking to the spiritual disciplines for proof that we're right. Recovery comes when our prayers and reflections move from "Lord, protect me from my enemies," to "Lord, help me learn from this." It's exchanging one vulnerability for another and being open to the possibility that God may speak to us in complaint. As Dietrich Bonhoeffer, the martyred German theologian, noted, "The more we learn to allow others to speak the word to us, to accept humbly and gratefully even severe reproaches and admonitions, the more free and objective will we be in speaking ourselves."[3]

This kind of spiritual listening does not happen overnight, or without a grinding inner struggle. But it does happen, and when it does we may see things differently. Remember, for the most part we have had a lifetime of receiving criticism and feeling terrible. The point of this discussion is that feeling terrible usually comes with getting criticized. That fact will not change today or tomorrow. But we can enter into the defensiveness cycle better prepared with understandings and tools to deal with the stresses, confident that through it all we'll be OK.

NOTES

1. Wayne E. Oates, *The Care of Troublesome People* (Bethesda: Alban, 1994); Peter Steinke, *How Your Church Family Works: Understanding Congregations as Emotional Systems* (Bethesda: Alban, 1993); Lloyd Rediger, "Managing the Clergy Killer Phenomenon," *The Clergy Journal* (March 1994).

2. Henri J. M. Nouwen, *The Genesee Diary: Report from a Trappist Monastery* (Garden City, N.Y.: Doubleday & Co., 1976), 57.

3. Dietrich Bonhoeffer, *Life Together* (London: SCM Press Ltd., 1963), 96.

Originally published in Congregations: The Alban Journal *21, no. 6 (November/ December 1995): pp. 5-7.*

CHAPTER 9

Neutralizing a History

George D. Parsons

Back in the days when we could still build an open campfire on the trail, my friends and I, after a long day's hike, would settle in for a relaxing evening around the fire, singing and telling stories. The campfire was the focal point for our relating and a symbol of our connection to one another. Of all the beauties and pleasures of backpacking it is the time spent around the fire that I remember most.

On one such occasion I remember smothering the fire at evening's end with sand and discovering the next morning as I cleared the fire pit that some embers continued to burn underneath—enough so that I could start a new fire. This is the analogy that comes to mind when I see caring relationships damaged in church conflicts. It is as if a good fire is buried under sand—either slowly, one handful at a time, or quickly, in an avalanche of shovel loads—so that it is apparently extinguished. A relationship that was once warm and illuminating is now a dull pile of resentments, hurts, and disappointments.

When a relationship reaches this point, piled high with pain and anger, the people involved will ask the revokability question. Can we take back what we have said or done? Is recovery possible? Can we go forward together in this relationship? But the question is difficult to answer when all that one sees is the smoldering pile. When one's perspective is captive to the accumulation of hurts, the answer is usually, "No, too much has happened, I am too hurt, too angry to go on!" Being able to assess revokability requires a changed perspective, to see below the sand to what may be left in the fire pit. The requirement, in other words, is to set aside or neutralize the heap of emotions built up over time so that the parties may see more clearly what is left from which a relationship may or may not be rekindled. I assist people to do this by employing a strategy called "neutralizing history," first developed by Dr. Susan K. Gilmore at the University of Oregon as a marriage counseling intervention. The strategy is most useful in church conflicts where significant relationships—between two staff members, between a pastor and a parishioner, or between two parishioners—have been damaged in the conflict.

The word *neutralize* is quite descriptive of the purposes of this intervention. Since it is not known if the relationship in question can survive and in fact the two people involved are by no means sure that they even want to *try* to recover—it makes no sense to have as an initial goal the rebuilding of the relationship. Instead, the purpose here is to neutralize the negative history so that, by setting history aside, both parties can take a look at the possibilities and can more readily determine what it is they want to do.

PREPARATION

Often when a relationship is broken, one party has amassed a much larger pile of painful history than the other. When this is the case I ask that person to prepare for a face-to-face meeting by first working alone to recall the events in the relationship that created the pain. I then ask him or her to record in advance a brief description of these events on 3 x 5 cards, one event per card, followed by a brief description of the emotional impact of those events. A typical card might read like this:

> *Event*: "When I went to you [my pastor] to tell you how unhappy I was with the way you related to me and with the situation in our church generally, you suggested that I might be happier elsewhere and should consider leaving."
> *Impact*: "I felt rebuffed by you. I was seeking understanding and instead got a 'quick-fix' suggestion which left me feeling hurt and disappointed."

The person brings these cards to the meeting so that the cards become a shorthand version of what is communicated to the other person. If both parties have amassed pain and resentment, then both write out these cards in advance.

The other party, the one who will be hearing the information taken from the cards, will be prepared to provide good listening and understanding.

I give a quick lesson in paraphrasing since it is the most effective way to acknowledge understanding to another person. Understanding makes it possible to set aside a negative history when the one recounting pain has experienced clear evidence that the listener understands what this was like and what the impact was on him or her. Only then is the way clear to set aside the transgressions and look at what may be left of the relationship.

THE MEETING

With me present, the "wronged party" is encouraged to share the material on the cards, chronologically if possible, and the listener does nothing but paraphrase the history that is told. Even though the listener is going to hear information with which he or she disagrees, this will be a one-sided conversation. I discourage attempts to "correct the record" or get the facts straight. The purpose here is to focus on the emotional history, the emotional memory, of the one who has accumulated the pile. How that person remembers the events is all that matters, and so what is said is taken at face value as the listener works to understand the impact of the events on the speaker. The ground rules that I encourage in this meeting allow only for history sharing and paraphrasing. (There will be time later for questions, for the seeking and giving of forgiveness, and for problem solving.)

As the material from a card is spoken and adequately understood, I ask to take the card as a symbol of that person's willingness to let go of that piece of history. When the pile of cards is exhausted, we are finished unless the listener also has prepared some cards, in which case the roles are reversed and the process repeated.

This is a difficult and painful experience since it requires the reliving of old hurts for both the speaker and the listener. The listener, even if she or he hears no new information in the history, must endure the laundry list of perceived transgressions without defense. The speaker must risk telling it all, no punches pulled. Thus people are not likely to agree to this exchange unless (1) the relationship has been important to both; (2) you as a consultant and they are willing to give over the time (a neutralizing history meeting can last several hours); and (3) both parties trust the consultant to lead them through such an encounter.

Time must elapse before the effects of this process are apparent. I don't know why, but often the speaker may need a week or longer to begin to feel sufficiently unburdened of the history to be able to look at the future of the relationship. But the strategy has repeatedly cleared the way for a new decision and provided a foundation upon which to build forgiveness and new hope. When that happens I respond the way I did that morning on the hiking trail—with humility in the face of the seemingly unexpected and with awe at the power of God's grace.

Originally published in Action Information *14, no. 4 (July/August 1988): pp. 5-6.*

CHAPTER 10

Recovering from a Church Fight: Talking across the Old Lines

George D. Parsons

Someone once observed that conflict in the church seems to be a team sport. They were referring, of course, to the predictable development of "clump" or factions within a congregation as the level of conflict increases. In chapter 9 of this book, I discussed the use of the "neutralizing history" technique when two individuals have accumulated a history of negative feelings. This process can be an initial step toward rebuilding a damaged relationship. But what can be done when painful history has developed between groups of people? Can we help the people who have been in factions to begin rebuilding relationships across those factional lines?

These questions take on more significance considering the difficulty many churches have as they try to recover from traumatic conflicts. When the aftermath of the fight is ignored, congregations enter a defensive retreat. Organizationally, this retreat is expressed in a lack of vision for the future, an inordinate amount of effort given to the maintenance of the church, and the suppression of difference, especially within the governing board of the congregation. Interpersonally, the retreat manifests itself in reduced contact among some people, or contact maintained at a more superficial level.

A defensive retreat becomes a separate peace (or a "Level Zero" conflict) in which people are quick to claim that the conflicts are past history and no longer worthy of discussion. People often say, "That is history now. We no longer need to talk about that," or "What's the use in dredging up old hurts and raking up discontent again?" This denial, which takes both organizational and individual forms, is very much like that described in Dennis and Matthew Linn's *Healing Life's Hurts*.[1] The Linns point out that all of us have a tendency to deny that we carry with us the results of the past in the form of hurt, anger, or guilt. While these emotional memories easily have the power to disrupt our individual and collective life, the invitation to address them usually brings strong resistance.

When a congregation begins to feel the effects of a defensive retreat (declining attendance, declining program, factional lines reemerging in a search committee or on the board) the leadership may begin to seek outside help. As a consultant in this situation, I begin by creating a liaison team made up of people from the various groups or factions in the earlier conflicts and ask this team to generate a list of people who were either most affected by the conflicts or were key leaders in the factions. From this list I help the team create small groups which include people from both or all the factions involved. The team then recruits people to participate in these small-group meetings which will be led by the consultant.

The team is prepared to meet the resistance from their "recruits" by speaking to the primary purpose of the small-group meetings, which is to help set the stage for the next era in the congregation's life. The purpose is *not* to rehash the old issues but to provide a safe place where people can begin to understand one another's hurt and anger and to open the way for reconciliation. The focus of this group is not issues but relationships.

Here is a typical sequence that such a small group might follow as they seek to address what happened in their relationships:

1. *A welcome and time for introductions.*
2. *A discussion of purpose.* Setting a stage for reconciliation.
3. *Creating a safe climate.* Henri Nouwen's concept of hospitality[2] is presented along with a brief practice in paraphrasing.
4. *Re-establishing common ground.* Participants are involved in a dialogue conversation about the roots of their faith and common experiences out of their life in the church together. (Most of the people in these small groups have known each other for a long time. These long-term relationships are what make hurt and anger run deeper.)
5. *Telling the stories, telling the pain.* People are asked to talk about their experience in the congregation (in pairs), to identify key events and the emotional impact of those events. Their partner paraphrases to acknowledge understanding and to enable the story to be told. Both have a chance to "tell their story" in this manner.
6. *Reporting to the group.* Aspects of the stories and emotional impact are discussed in the small group as a whole. (New information usually emerges during this time, since all factional fighting inhibits the flow of information and increases distortion in communication.)

7. *Exploring forgiveness.* We cannot *will* trust or reconciliation to oc-
    cur, but we can choose to give or seek forgiveness. People have an
    opportunity to reflect here on what they want from one another (while
    being encouraged to avoid superficial expressions of forgiveness).
8. *Pulling learnings from the fight.* The group is asked to reflect on
    what was learned through their experience with the conflict and what
    parts of that learning they would like to communicate to the board or
    congregation. Examples might be: "We have had dysfunctional rules
    [norms] about conflict and need to rewrite them so that we can talk
    more openly," or "This meeting has been useful for us but we want to
    involve more people in this kind of conversation."
9. *Confession, thanksgiving, and prayer.* A time of worship where
    opportunity is given to each person to acknowledge what they have
    contributed to the conflicts and where they feel truly thankful for those
    who have been "across the line" from them.

In some congregations we have set up committees that are equipped to
facilitate this kind of conversation at least one-on-one with people who for
various reasons were not involved in the small-group meetings. The consultant may return in six months to do a follow-up meeting, either with some
of the same participants or with a new group if necessary.

There is no magic in this approach, except for the working of God's
grace. People begin to talk across the lines (in many cases for the first
time). There is human contact and good listening. There is reaffirmation of
a shared desire to move forward as a congregation and there is a remembering of common ground. All of this sets a stage for reconciliation—but
reconciliation itself seems to happen in God's time, not our own.

NOTES

1. Dennis Linn and Matthew Linn, *Healing Life's Hurts: Healing Memories
through the Five Stages of Forgiveness* (Mahwah, N.J.: Paulist Press, 1988).
2. Henri J. M. Nouwen, *Reaching Out: The Three Movements of the Spiritual
Life* (New York: Image Books, 1986).

Originally published in Action Information *15, no. 3 (May/June 1989): pp. 13-14.*

CHAPTER 11

A Language of Caring Spoken Here

George D. Parsons

One summer a young female student was riding her bike home from the University of Oregon campus in Eugene. It was rush hour in that medium-sized community and the bicyclist was maneuvering through the usual morass of traffic. She was struck from behind by an inattentive driver and thrown to the side of the road, her leg fractured by the fall. Drivers slowed to gawk but no one stopped to help. Finally, after 15 minutes, a grocery store clerk looking out the store window saw the injured rider and came to her rescue.

This is familiar stuff for us. It is referred to as the "unresponsive bystander phenomenon" and is frequently reported in the newspapers of our communities, large and small. The most famous example may be the 1963 murder of Kitty Genovese in Queens, New York. These occurrences have been the topic of much research in the past 30 years and have led to some helpful insights about human behavior in general and specifically about our capacity to respond to others in caring ways.

Of the many conclusions drawn from the research on unresponsiveness, I would highlight these three:

1. It is easy to misperceive a situation and literally not see it as an opportunity to help.

2. The connection between values and behavior is easily broken, particularly by certain environmental factors that can lead caring people to believe that responding won't make any difference.

3. Most acts of caring require a performance. Even if we see an opportunity to help and believe that we could make a difference we may be stymied by performance anxiety or by not knowing what to say or do in a given situation.

These ideas have broad implications for our society, especially for public education, but my focus here is on helping congregations to put faithful purposes into caring action. There are learnings that we can draw from these conclusions, learnings that can assist us to be more caring communities of faith and more skillful in our handling of difference and disagreement.

All three of the research conclusions listed above point to the need for the development of caring skills, whether these be perceptual skills that enable us to see opportunities, cognitive skills that help us remember that we do make a difference, or social skills that enable us to speak a language of caring. For the scope of this essay, I wish to focus on the social-skill component and its application in our churches.

Since the primary language of our society is one of aggression, self-interest, competition, and hostility, putting our faith into action requires that we learn to speak a second, "foreign language," as it were. This idea is familiar to us as Christians, who follow a vision that is by definition counter-cultural. The world's values are not ours. Our society's predominant language is not a language of caring and so we seek a place where caring is spoken, where peacemaking and faith are shared and encouraged. Thus we see the church ideally as a center of caring to which we come remembering that we are "in the world but not of it." In Paul's list of the fruits of the Spirit appears the word *agathasune*, which is usually translated "goodness." A more accurate translation might be "virtue-equipped." Goodness is equipped to address a world with other values and priorities. Part of the equipment is a language of caring—caring skills that can be exercised in the church and in the world. Speaking a language of caring is not valued by the world at large, so we need some place where that language is shared and encouraged. For me that place is the church.

CARING AND CONFLICT

Conflict in a congregation may profoundly challenge this notion of the church as a center of caring. We wonder if our deeply held assumptions are valid and we certainly may begin to question whether the church can be the bearer of good news, speaking a language of caring in an uncaring world. The gap between our idealized view of the church and the realities of church life, made so apparent when conflict emerges, lead us to fear conflict, to want to avoid issues, and to fall into defensive retreat and despair. Yet so often I have heard people in congregations say, after working through a difficult conflict, that they have a renewed belief in the church's capacity to care and a renewed confidence in their own ability to reach out to others during a crisis. What makes the difference? I would say acquiring and applying a language of caring, a language that helps set the stage for God's grace to work in our corporate life.

There are a multitude of skills in a language of caring, some as simple as a first grader learning to say to his parent, "How was your day?" or a church member's response to a visitor at worship, "I'd like to welcome you and offer my help in getting to know our church." Other skills are more complex, such as the verbal skills required in a collaborative problem-solving strategy, or making clear purpose and preference statements. I want to provide one example of the language of caring, a skill that can play a profound role in the life of a congregation.

If you come to my home to visit, I usually extend my right hand and clear off the couch (where my children's belongings pile up) so that you have room to sit. This is intended as an act of hospitality, to make space for you in my home. Henri Nouwen, in his book *Reaching Out*, writes eloquently of the role that hospitality might play in our lives. He tells the following Zen story:

> Nan-in, a Japanese master during the Meiji era (1868-1912), received a university professor who came to inquire about Zen. Nan-in served tea. He poured his visitor's cup full, and then kept pouring. The professor watched the overflow until he could no longer restrain himself. "It is overfull. No more will go in!" "Like this cup, "Nan-in said, "You are full of your opinions and speculations. How can I show you Zen unless you first empty your cup?"[1]

A language of caring requires that we know how to clear a space within ourselves, to allow room for the other person's concerns and for their story. A key skill, therefore, in the language of caring, is paraphrasing—to say back briefly in your own words what another is saying. It is a skill infrequently used in day-to-day life and a skill poorly taught. Yet what it provides is so desperately needed, especially when there is conflict. Taking the time to restate an adversary's point of view, and therefore to convey one's understanding of the other, is a precious gift that can lessen hostility and build a foundation for working through disagreements.

Here are some paraphrases I've heard in the midst of church conflicts:

- "So you are feeling that the decision to use inclusive language in worship will cause some of your friends to pull away from the church."
- "You are convinced that my view of the pastor's performance is inaccurate in some ways."
- "It sounds like you felt that you couldn't come to me directly with your complaint because I wouldn't understand."
- "These difficulties have been so painful for you that you're not sure you can stay in the church."

Paraphrasing is an elegant form of hospitality that can open the way for collaboration or negotiation or reconciliation. But when it is absent, so is understanding, and good conflict management is not likely to prevail. Of course, like most every other element in a language of caring, paraphrasing is little used in our society and sounds foreign to the ear. But it can be learned and practiced just as one would master a musical instrument, an athletic endeavor, or an intellectual pursuit. And what better place to learn and practice this foreign language than in the church?

I can easily imagine hanging a sign over the doorways of our congregations that says, "A LANGUAGE OF CARING SPOKEN HERE." The sign would mean that in this place the world's values do not hold forth and neither does a fear of conflict. The sign would mean that in this place love rules and we know how to speak our love. The sign over the door would mean that we are the people of God, equipping ourselves so that faith finds its expression within our walls and out in the world.

NOTE

1. Henri J. M. Nouwen, *Reaching Out: The Three Movements of the Spiritual Life* (New York: Image Books, 1986), p. 54.

Originally published in Action Information *13, no. 2 (March/April 1987): pp. 1-3.*

CHAPTER 12

Who's at Fault
When the Pastor Gets Fired?

Speed B. Leas

*For what was happening, I can grasp now, was the misjudg-
ment greater by far than their decision to be married: their
mutual refusal to call it off. Each had a fear blockading that
logical retreat. Dad would not admit his mistake because he
wanted not to look a fool to the valley. On that he was entirely
wrong; the only mystification anyone seemed to have was why
he kept on with a hopeless mismatch. . . . For her part, Ruth
would not face up to another split, would not let another broken marriage point to her as an impossible wife.*[1]

So writes Ivan Doig of his father and stepmother in *This House of Sky*.
He sees, as an outsider, that this is a bad relationship. The insiders,
however, because of their own needs to appear to themselves and others as
righteous, cannot admit their mistake, but must find enough fault with the
other to justify taking the initiative to terminate the relationship. Some clergy
and congregations get into the same bind. They know it's a bad match:
staying together isn't good for the pastor or the congregation. But how does
it end? A reason must be found, a justification, a fault.

When the Alban Institute undertook a study of congregations where
the pastor had been fired, we started our research with exactly the same
kind of question: Whose fault was it? While we could find some situations
that were primarily the congregation's "fault" (a congregation that wanted
a pastor to work with young people hired a clergyman who explicitly, and in
writing, said that he did not want to work with young people), and we
could find some that were primarily the pastor's "fault" (the pastor
stopped calling on members and stopped attending any church meetings),
these occurrences were rare. Most of the time we found a mixture of

congregational and pastoral causes that defied unraveling as to who "started it." Asking the question "Whose fault is it?" in the church seemed to tangle people up (including the executives and the consultants) more than it helped bring purposeful action to the situation. A much more helpful question is: "Do these people want to live, work, and be in ministry together?"

When one approaches the problem of conflict management from the perspective of finding out who is at fault (or who is mostly at fault), one is forced to respond to the situation in a way that seeks punishment for the "wrongdoer" and vindication for those who were in the "right." In our research into 127 "involuntary terminations" or firings, we found the need to find fault to be one of the most characteristic and least helpful dimensions of the conflict, frequently leading to increasing the hurts and confusions for everybody concerned.

In fact, we found that it is almost never the case that one party is exclusively in the wrong. We came to see that when troubles arise between some members and the pastor, the first question should be, "Can we find a way to work things out so that this relationship can again become rewarding?" If the parties are not able to arrive at decisions they all find to be meaningful and useful, then, perhaps, the relationship should be broken.

Sometimes the breaking of this relationship does not seem to be fair—especially to clergy. But the key criterion for ministry has to do with charity, not with fairness. Instead of asking what is deserved, Christian charity asks the question about the possibility of ministry with this group of people—and that means the vast majority of them. Christian charity asks the question, "Do I love these people and want them to be served by a person or persons who can genuinely minister to their needs in their situation?" If the pastor feels good about being with the people, if she or he wants to continue living with them, if she or he wants to be deeply involved with them in their lives, if she or he wants to support them in their times of trouble and tribulation, then the motivation for staying is appropriate. The question is the same for the laity in the congregation. Can ministry be possible between them and this pastor? Or has the relationship been irreparably broken by what has happened, regardless of who is to blame?

If pastor and people can see the possibility of ministering together, grace and hard work may restore something better than had been there previously (in Alban's studies of long-tenured pastors we discovered that many of the finest long pastorates were marked by at least one sharp clergy/lay fight in its earlier years). If both agree that the will to continue is not there, we find that careful work can help a dissolution of relationship to occur without major damage to pastor and laity. When there is no unanimity on that point, much more skillful, time-consuming work is needed to keep people from hurting each other in long-lasting ways.

It is very difficult for the pastor to look at this question of the possibility of ministry (rather than the issue of fairness) when one has children who haven't finished at this high school, or when one is concerned about the possibility of finding another comparable job, or when one has poured out his or her heart and soul giving the best she or he knows how to give, and hears these sorts of responses: the sermons are too long, you have bad taste in clothes, don't you think it's time to move on? The responses seem unfair (and may so be), but the issue remains: Is it possible for this person to minister, in this place, to these people?

Is it thinkable in a Christian church for a group of people consciously to terminate their relationship with another person? I think the New Testament answer is: sometimes yes, after people have worked very, very hard at trying to make a go of the relationship. In the New Testament there are a variety of sayings and stories that indicate Jesus did not believe that it was always possible for relationships to continue indefinitely. Sometimes it was necessary to recognize that folks needed to give up trying to find ways to stay together. In Matthew and Mark and twice in Luke, Jesus is quoted as saying that if people don't listen to your words, shake off the dust from your feet as you leave that house or town. It is a clear message that when you are not accepted, go elsewhere; do not endlessly strive to get through to the other.

It needs to be pointed out, however, that this advice is to be understood in the context of repeated attempts to make the relationship work. In Matthew 18 the advice is to try several different ways to work things out (alone, with one or two helpers, then with the assistance of the church). Clearly the admonitions to turn the other cheek, to go an extra mile, to give cloak and coat, to forgive seventy times seven times, and to forgive those who repent after they have sinned (even seven times in a day) are all profound calls to do everything within your power to make a relationship work—one is not to casually seek an end or walk out of communion with other people. Nonetheless, after significant struggle, the day may come when separation may be better than alienated living together.

Confronting this possibility of separation can push people into their religious dimension in a way that few other experiences are able to do. (This phrase "pushing people into their religious dimension" came to Marty Saarinen as he helped me reflect on my learnings from this research.) Where an involuntary termination becomes a possibility, clergy perceive themselves to be in a situation of professional survival with the sense of security which has come from their own accomplishments now being knocked out from under them. Where, before the threat of termination, a pastor might have believed in skill and learning and hard work as the foundations of acceptability before others and God, now this person may be pushed toward a faith beyond self-reliance.

Not only does this experience call persons to affirm their dependence on God in a profound way, but it also tests their abilities to respond to others (especially those perceived as enemies) in ways that affirm Christian morality. Pastors are in particularly difficult situations at this point. Not only do they need to marshal all their resources to manage themselves, their fears, and their angers; they need also to have strength to help manage those people who are supporting them. In conflict they are tempted (like everybody else) to blame, attack, punish, and get rid of those with whom they disagree. Their supporters often move toward the "dissidents" with vicious and malevolent intent. Such a system of bolstering up the pastor and rallying around his or her survival escalates the difficulty into something which is disruptive not only for pastor and family, but the parish as well. Therefore, disruptive conflict pushes people into their religious dimension in that it calls for responsible use of Christian ethics, as well as reliance on God for strength when one is tempted to punish or destroy those who are on "the other side."

Laity are pushed into their religious dimension in the same ways. Though the professional stakes are not as high for them, certainly their standing in the community, their relations with persons who heretofore were friends, and their concern for the maintenance of the local church are all strained and called to judgment before these trying experiences. Moreover, often laity are thrust into the position of attempting to love another person and at the same time speak words of chastisement and judgment to those with whom they disagree. Conflicting priorities and evaluations are bound with a net of caring and concern.

Denominational executives and consultants to churches in conflict are pushed into the religious dimension as well. To those who hurt they are called to bind wounds; to those who would seek to damage and punish they are called to set limits, chastise, and reform; and to those who despair (give up hope) they are called to witness to the possibilities of new life and an open future.

Situations involving the possibility of involuntary terminations, thus, can be opportunities for growth and religious development. Progress in these dimensions, however, is often not the outcome. From our studies, it is our perception that more often than not congregations, clergy, and executives actually lose hope, deny the openness of the future, and seek retaliation rather than newness of life. It is our hope that as we all learn more about ourselves and about the dynamics of disruptive conflict, we will be able to find in confrontation an opportunity to learn, in difference an appreciation of diversity, and in change (forced or chosen) an opportunity for freedom and life.

NOTE

1. Ivan Doig, *This House of Sky: Landscapes of a Western Mind* (New York: Harcourt Brace, 1977), p. 73.

Originally published in Action Information *6, no. 6 (November/December 1980): pp. 1-3.*

CHAPTER 13

How to Handle Complaints about Your Fellow Staff Member

Speed B. Leas

O nce, when leading a three-day conference in Wisconsin for multiple-staff teams, I heard from almost all of them the same problem: "What do you do when laity come backbiting the other pastor?" Two brief examples will illustrate the problem. In one case the senior pastor had a young man come to him and complain about how little prayer and spiritual focus there was in the youth group. The senior pastor and the associate had previously agreed not to interfere with each other's areas of responsibility. What was the senior pastor to do? He didn't want to "interfere," yet he also thought the associate might need to know how the young people felt about his ministry.

In another situation, the associate was invited to dinner by a prominent family in the congregation. She was told in great detail at the dinner how poorly the senior pastor ran council meetings and how incompetent he was as an administrator. The associate worried about what to do with this information. She didn't want to "tattle" on the family who had invited her to dinner, and she was very nervous about what the pastor might do if he heard about the bad feelings from this family. Sometimes in cases like this he would go into a mild depression and pout; at other times he would take his discomfort out on her, implying that she encouraged such discussions. What was she to do with this information?

We have learned from working with team ministries three courses of action that make matters worse in such situations:

- Commiserating with the "plaintiff" and keeping the information to yourself (the usual way these problems are handled)
- Pretending you agree with the "plaintiff" and then sharing the information with your teammate

- Agreeing with the person who is making the complaint, and sharing the data with other people in the congregation, but not with the other member of the staff

These three courses of action bring more difficulty. When you keep the comments to yourself, the people with complaints keep coming to you. Everybody's feelings of frustration are heightened, because you keep naming the problem, and nothing happens that might bring some hope of change. There isn't any relief for your feelings of dissatisfaction since you are not able to share them in settings that are likely to produce a catharsis.

Sharing the information with your teammate in secret is often disappointing because neither of you are in a position to do anything about the problem. So there it stays, stuck in both your craws.

Of course, sharing your information with others in the congregation who may be opposed to your "partner" is the poorest way to handle the situation. It increases everyone's anxiety. While the opponents may think your action will help them in the short run to meet their needs (to hurt, embarrass, or get rid of the pastor), in the long run they are fully aware that you are not a person who can be trusted. Moreover, secrecy, clandestine behavior, and manipulation will be behaviors that will be encouraged and supported by such actions.

What, then, can you do? First let us note that at the heart of the problem may be a norm or unwritten ground rule that it is not OK in this congregation to speak directly with a person with whom you have a grievance. The norm may be that it is appropriate to tell only a third party (clergy or laity) about your difficulty. This norm will always slow down, if not completely hamper, open communication in the congregation. One thing that you can do about this is to preach about the subject and help everyone in the congregation be aware of its problematic nature. Further, help people practice not telling third parties about their grievances unless they also tell the party with whom they have the difference. Early contracting between team members can also be important. The team members make a list of how they agree to deal with each other in all aspects of parish life. This list or contract should be published. In the list should be included the statement that outside of counseling situations, where it is assumed that all communications are privileged, everything that occurs in the professional setting or has to do with professional performance will be shared by the professional members of the team.

Just writing this in a covenant between staff members and publishing it will not be enough, however. Each staff member will be tested regularly as to his or her actual commitment to the covenant. When you are approached by a parishioner to play "ain't it awful" with regard to a teammate, it would be appropriate to say, "I am interested in hearing what you have to say about my associate, and I want to remind you that we have a covenant to share all concerns that are raised about the other person with names attached."

In other words, that which gets shared with you is not confidential except in counseling sessions. So many times clergy find themselves in awkward positions because they proclaim or imply that they can be "trusted," that all communication is privileged and will not go any further. They adopt a kind of conspiratorial stance or secretive posture and then often find themselves in a position where they "reveal" privileged information—such as Mabel was in the hospital to have a breast removed, and John's son, Bill, spent the night in jail on a drunk driving charge. A better posture is one which says we share each other's woes, each other's burdens bear.

A second thing that pastors can do when hearing complaints about their associate is to train persons with grievances to take their concerns to the offending party themselves. Such training might include encouraging the discontented person to share his or her concern directly, reminding the person that the other team members want to have such feedback, helping the person articulate clearly what the problem is, and letting the parishioner practice "confronting" the other team member in a semi-role play with you.

Third, help the complainer explore what might be keeping him or her from going directly to your partner. What is there to be afraid of? What fantasies does the person have about what might happen? Are those fantasies realistic?

Fourth, plan with the person when, where, and how to present the problem. Perhaps it's not a good idea to bring it up just before the pastor goes into the pulpit or in a reception line. You might be able to make some suggestions about when you think your colleague is most open to such a discussion and where to hold the conversation—at the church, a restaurant, or the plaintiff's home?

Fifth, it might help the person speak openly if you go, too. If the complainant indicates that it is too frightening to tell the other pastor about the problem, then offer to go along as a helper. In this case it might be a good idea to discuss with your partner the fact that this is going to happen or, better yet, plan for such a possibility ahead of time.

Finally, the person with the problem might find it helpful to dramatize or exaggerate his or her feelings with you. Sometimes the feelings are strong, but the issue is not major. Helping the person fully express the feelings to you may then allow the person to speak more rationally and appropriately with the other pastor. Don't assume that because strong feelings were expressed to you they will be that person's feelings for all time. Sometimes we need a chance to vent, before we can get things into perspective. Thus, once the person understands you will share concerns about issues with the other pastor, and that you want him or her to tell your colleague about those concerns, then it may be helpful to invite the person to share as fully with you as he or she would feel comfortable doing.

In short, backbiting is not an appropriate way to work in professional settings in the church. And it is not helpful just to listen to the problems and hope they will resolve themselves. I'm suggesting that you help other people manage their own conflicts. If possible, don't be a runner with others' grievances, but, if you are, make sure you carry no messages anonymously; make sure people know the consequences of their speaking to you and then hope they will take responsibility for their own complaints.

Originally published in Action Information *5, no. 2 (March /April 1979): pp. 6-7.*

PART THREE

Situational Conflict

CHAPTER 14

Managing Conflict in Yoked Parishes: A Case Study

Clinton A. McCoy

Two consistories sat opposite one another, one filled with certainty, the other with apprehension. Members of these small congregations, from the same sociological niche, thought they knew each other well. They had grown up in each other's communities and shared some extended family. The congregations had been yoked together in a stable and generally harmonious relationship, sharing the leadership of several pastors for over half a century. What brought the consistories together this night was an invitation by South Creek United Church of Christ to discuss the decision Homestead Hills U.C.C. had made to dissolve its relationship with the pastor, Reverend John Miller.

I had been working as consultant to mediate a serious conflict between Homestead Hills and the pastor. Interested in the process and intrigued by what was happening, about six weeks into the process the South Creek consistory inquired whether I might also work with their consistory and pastor. Ready to review data gathered from interviews, the Homestead consistory decided to be patient, allowing South Creek to begin their own process of consultation. The pastor was also anxious to have a more complete picture of his relationship to the two churches. Working independently with the consistory at South Creek, we were able to involve a significant number of members in an interview process, just as we had already done at Homestead Hills. Then, with the information gathered and organized, I met with each consistory on consecutive evenings to share the results.

At the meeting with the Homestead Hills consistory and pastor, the data were made known. They revealed that the pastor had lost virtually the entire base of support from church leaders and most of the congregation. Details of the data were summarized. After lengthy discussion and some confrontation, the consistory voted to recommend to the congregation that the relationship with the pastor be dissolved. Not only was this recommendation a surprise to the pastor, it was a surprise to me as well. I believed that after being paired for 65 years with a neighboring congregation, Homestead Hills would at least delay its decision until it had heard from, or consulted with, South Creek. In fact, out of respect for the South Creek friends, they said they did not want Homestead's problems to contaminate South Creek's relationship to the pastor. They agreed, however, to share their decision with the South Creek consistory, who would be asked to keep the information confidential.

It was, understandably, a gun-shy pastor who met with the South Creek consistory and me the following night. As the meeting opened, I noted the decision that the Homestead Hills consistory had made, but revealed that more than 70 percent of the members of the South Creek church, including most of the leaders, supported the pastor. I indicated that some dissatisfaction with the pastor's performance had been expressed, including some sharp criticism by the pastor's supporters. But the congregation was being patient and on the whole appreciated Reverend Miller's work among them. Questions and discussion by the South Creek consistory revealed that its members were bewildered and confused. "What are we supposed to do," asked Walt, "just let Homestead Hills make this decision for us? Is Reverend Miller willing to serve us part-time, or will he be forced out?" The pastor indicated that he would consider a part-time position.

"We need to talk to Homestead," said Bonnie. "Our churches have been yoked together for so long and have shared so much, I can't imagine dissolving the yoke. Why didn't they speak to us before they took this action? Don't they care about us and what we think?"

At this point the South Creek leaders decided to invite the Homestead Hills leaders to meet with them in special joint session. When they came together Homestead's leaders put their decision on the table: they had decided that they could no longer support the pastor and his ministry. The base of support in the church had dried up to almost nothing; worship attendance was lower than it had ever been; the pastor did not have the support of any recognized leader in the congregation. In fact, none of the elected leaders had voted to recommend in his favor. Homestead answered South Creek's questions directly but were immovable in their resolve.

"Did you just think you could make this decision and we would go along?" asked South Creek's Bill.

"We just assumed you would see things the same way we do," said Nancy from Homestead. "None of us wants to dissolve the yoke."

With no new information to share and not intending to change their position, Homestead's representatives left the South Creek leaders struggling to decide what it was they would do. "It looks like we have two choices," said Elaine. "Either we recommend to the congregation that the pastoral relationship be dissolved, or we recommend that the yoke be dissolved. Neither decision is acceptable to me."

"I still don't like it that they think they can make a decision for us," said Walt.

"I am surprised by the diversity of responses to the pastor in our congregation," said Ruth, who was not one of his greatest advocates. "Reverend Miller has more support than I realized."

As the South Creek consistory considered this dilemma, a third alternative surfaced. They realized that if they chose simply to continue being a half-time pastorate served by the pastor, they could endorse consultant recommendations to pursue a process with the pastor to settle accountability issues, encourage the pastor to secure more training in areas of weakness, and ultimately place the responsibility for the decision to dissolve the yoke with the Homestead consistory. "That's where the responsibility belongs," one of South Creek's leaders said.

Surprised by the South Creek action, the Homestead leaders immediately called the consultant to advise that they were not sure that the congregation would sustain their recommendation if it meant dissolving the relationship between the churches. But after a few days of internal consultation, it was decided that the best, though painful, decision for the future of the congregation would be to dissolve the pastoral relationship and to try to secure some other way of providing part-time pastoral service.

And so it was these two congregations with so much in common, including over 50 years of cooperative service, began a process of separation. In a subsequent interview with the Homestead consistory, members indicated to me that they hoped that sometime in the future they might again be yoked with South Creek. They could not believe that the South Creek people didn't feel the same exasperation with the pastor that they did. Their words reflected the hurt of separation. I wondered whether the legacy of their conflict with the pastor would be an open wound for them as long as he continued with their former partners in South Creek. Certainly their relief that a decision had been made, and the separation proceedings set in process, was tempered by sadness.

ANALYZING THE SCENARIO

This scenario illustrates that when it comes to the ways conflict affects congregations yoked together, it is wise not to make assumptions. In the case described above, I believed that the solid, long-term relationship between South Creek and Homestead Hills would supply enough pressure to encourage the Homestead leaders to be more patient with their pastor, to give him opportunity to improve his skills, hone his leadership capabilities, and develop closer ties with the membership and the community. I was dead wrong.

I also believed, having been invited by South Creek to consult with them, that the two churches, so similar in size and geographical area served, would have the same complaints against the pastor, made with the same level of intensity. Once again I was wrong.

What were the factors that precipitated church leaders to reach such different conclusions about their relationship to the pastor? Besides issues of personality, the differences had to do with the age of church participants, particularly the presence of children, the financial condition of each congregation, their hopes for what this new young pastor could do for them, and, in some measure, where the pastor lived.

1. *Age of members.* Homestead's congregation is graying significantly. Scanning the first seven names on the membership list, one member noted that six of those people are shut-in. Most members are retired. The one family with children who had been attending worship had taken their children to South Creek where they could join with other parents in providing a Sunday School program.

South Creek's congregation, on the other hand, has a good age mix and most of the consistory members are close in age to the pastor. The woman who is recognized by most as the outstanding church leader (she is not on the consistory) is a grandmother in her fifties who has the trust of both the youngest and oldest folk in the congregation. It is not insignificant that she likes the pastor! Most of the pastor's detractors at South Creek are older members, along with another couple who have relatives in Homestead who are deeply involved in the conflict.

2. *The presence of children.* Children are an indicator of the future, an indicator of hope. A lament heard over and over again in Homestead is that there are no young people. Without young children to whom to tell

a children's sermon, that the pastor dropped part of the weekly worship service, which disturbed people. "There is no one to tell a children's sermon to," the pastor says. There is a person to lead the Homestead Hills children's choir, but no one to sing.

On the other hand, the Sunday School program and choir at South Creek are thriving, with an average of 25 children present in Sunday School. The attitude at South Creek is positive. Many members enjoy the children's time during worship, conducted by the pastor.

3. *Financial stability.* The Homestead leaders reported that they had to dip deeply into their savings last year and, with a decline in membership and accompanying pledges, they will be out of money in less than two years if the present course continues unchanged.

Although the South Creek church is not wealthy, they are paying their bills. They are uncertain whether, if the yoke is continued, the Homestead Hills congregation will be able to hold up their end of the covenant in the future, and this concerns them. "What will you be able to do next year?" they asked Homestead representatives in joint session. The answer they received was not reassuring.

4. *Realistic expectations for the pastor's performance.* The Homestead congregation had hoped that a young pastor (a phenomenon they had not experienced for some time) would help them attract new and young members, but that had not happened. They had hoped that a young pastor would also attract neighborhood children, but neither had that happened.

The South Creek leaders were, of course, less anxious about the pastor's bringing in children, although they were interested in his attracting new members. Rather than seeing his inexperience as a liability, they seemed to expect possible growing pains. Instead of comparing his performance unfavorably to that of his predecessor, whom many loved and admired, at South Creek the pastor was seen as inexperienced and still learning, "the difference between a master and a rookie," said the daughter of the South Creek matriarch. Many expected that this new pastor would have a lot to learn; making mistakes was a part of learning. South Creek had less to lose than Homestead Hills; they felt they could be more patient.

5. *Parsonage location.* Although most interview respondents did not believe parsonage location played a part in their perception, comments implied that changing the location of the pastor's home from Homestead Hills to South Creek had a mild impact. "I suggested that he come to the Homestead post office and greet people like Reverend Jamison used to do when

he picked up his mail," said one respondent from Homestead Hills. When young Reverend Miller went to the Homestead post office as was suggested, he felt like a politician looking for votes. People go to the post office to pick up their mail or to buy stamps, not to meet the pastor. No one was there to introduce him to anyone; he didn't know exactly what to say. He felt foolish. People came in and gave him funny looks. The postmaster said he was embarrassed by his pastor just standing there.

In South Creek, however, a mother noted that the pastor had attended one of her children's ball games, and it was good to have him so visible in the community. "I don't remember seeing Reverend Jamison travel down here for ball games," she said. "I think those people are mad that we have a pastor living down here rather than up there," said one older supporter of the pastor who participated in the first negotiations over parsonage location more than 50 years ago. The perceptions indicated that at least pastoral visibility and a sense of the pastor's belonging to a community were important factors that affected people's perceptions.

GUIDANCE FOR YOKED PARISHES

It is with caution that one generalizes from particulars, but the following are commonsense guides for people who work with or plan to work with yoked parishes:

a. Do not expect one congregation to think like the other, no matter how alike they may seem at first blush nor how similar in character the communities they serve seem to be.

b. Yoked churches really are organizational subsystems of an informal, larger system. They each deserve to be consulted by the other when decisions made by one affect the interests of the other.

c. There are many kinds of "glue" which may hold yoked congregations together, among them financial necessity, the love of a pastor, a jointly held sense of mission and purpose, long-standing tradition, and so forth. It is very important that a functional parish council be established to work on personnel and other intracongregational issues that affect the interests of each. The more a parish council is influenced by pastoral control, the less effective it will be when the pastor is involved in conflict with one congregation or the other.

d. It is predictable that a congregation feeling stressed by aging members, declining participation, and financial difficulty will feel more intensely disappointed by unrealized expectations and will have a lower tolerance of anything that challenges the congregation's viability. In a multipoint parish, pastors and church leaders must be aware that all relationships are interdependent, meaning that the fears of one congregation will ultimately affect the life of the other.

e. If one congregation calls in a consultant for assistance, almost certainly the other congregation will be intrigued by what is happening, and have questions that need to be answered. This needs to be anticipated. Beyond this, the initiating congregation needs, early in the process, to decide at what level to communicate with the partner congregation about the basic process in which they are engaging, and decide in what ways the leaders of both congregations can find mutual ground for making decisions. The mutual interests of Homestead Hills and South Creek churches might have been better served had the consistories reached early agreement that no independent decision would be taken before a mutual consultation was held.

f. When a separation of a yoke occurs, each congregation will grieve, and all of the dynamics of grief will surface: shock, confusion, panic, helplessness, guilt, sadness, depression, anger, resentment, and, eventually, hope. Nevertheless, the congregations will grieve unevenly, depending on who loses most. Someone (a consultant, interim minister, executive, or other appropriate person, depending on the denomination's support structure) needs to help each congregation work through the grieving and come to terms with how the congregations envision themselves continuing their ministry and mission, no longer as family, but as neighbors.

Finally, it is often an unwritten rule, regardless of the denomination, that our least experienced pastors serve the smallest congregations, which are yoked together because yoking is one way these churches are able to afford pastoral service and pay a livable salary to a person with professional competence. The irony is that it is this very service which often demands a very high level of organizational knowledge and group process skill from the pastor. Yoked congregations interviewing prospective ministers should ask what continuing education they have had in group process and organization development. Judicatory executives, personnel committees, and others who are involved in the assignment process for pastors would do well to encourage these clergy to give priority to the enhancement of their group process skills.

Originally published in Action Information *18, no. 2 (March/April 1992): pp. 6-9.*

CHAPTER 15

Managing Conflict in African American Congregations

Ernest W. Walker

Perhaps no other institution has been of more importance to the African American community in the United States than the church. From its inception in slavery to the present day, it has been and continues to be the repository of African American culture, tradition, and faith. In addition, the African American church remains a refuge for a people who daily experience the assaults of a society that devalues them, and in some cases seeks to destroy them. The church remains a place where they can truly experience God's love—given freely and joyously to all. Like any other institution, the African American church is subject to conflict. The nature of the conflict varies depending on whether the church is *connectional* (tied to a white mainline denomination) or *independent* (having its own governing body).

This essay is in part the result of discussions with African American pastors of varying denominations and my own work as a consultant with churches having significant African American memberships. Although the dynamics of power, culture, and race play out differently in predominantly African American congregations and mixed congregations (white and African American), they nevertheless are significant factors.

Here I will discuss the roles that power, culture, and race play in African American connectional congregations. I will use as examples three churches with which I consulted, though the names and locations have been changed for the sake of confidentiality.

POWER

Connectional African American congregations are reflections of the denominations to which they belong. They share polity, liturgy, and music.

In some instances, these are "mission" churches that do not generate enough income to sustain themselves; they thus receive some or significant financial support from the denomination. African American parishioners in connectional congregations sometimes wrestle with issues of low self-esteem, wish for self-determination, and feel a sense of powerlessness; members feel their destiny is not their own. This sense of low self-esteem is directly related to the long-term dependence in relationships with the white church's power structure.

These churches also tend to be in transitional neighborhoods, with a former white constituency having moved from the inner city to the suburbs. Some members who have remained may take inappropriate steps to empower themselves. They may attack the pastor, organize factions among the other parishioners, or ingratiate themselves with the denomination as a means of taking power in the congregation.

In a mixed congregation of European Americans and African Americans there may be a power struggle between the two groups. The European American membership may represent a time when the church was all white and may still hold the reins of power even if it is in the minority. The African American membership may be relatively new to the church and have little influence or power. The white members may be uncomfortable with an African American pastor and work to undermine his or her authority. This was the case at High Street Lutheran Church.

High Street Lutheran is located in an inner-city neighborhood in a large, West Coast urban area. The church, although largely African American, identifies itself as multicultural because there are a significant number of Latino parishioners. Years ago the church began as a Swedish congregation, but as time passed whites moved out and the neighborhood became more African American and Latino. The church was struggling financially, its growth was stagnant, and there was very little outreach to the surrounding community. Even as the church changed color the pastors did not. The church had its first African American pastor in 1989 and its second in 1993. In addition to the African American and Latino congregants, a significant number of whites remained, some of who were long-time members. Shortly after the second African American pastor was called, an apparent power struggle ensued between him and some white members.

A group of white church members held clandestine meetings without the pastor's knowledge or involvement. Issues discussed at these meetings included complaints regarding his leadership and the administration of the church. A retired pastor, who had previously served as an interim in the congregation, also attended these meetings. Further exacerbating the conflict, the retired pastor performed a baptism in the senior pastor's absence without his knowledge or permission. Matters became unmanageable.

CULTURE

The role of culture in African American churches cannot be overemphasized. Some mainline denominations, in an effort to reach out to African American congregations, have recruited seminarians who were formerly members of independent denominations where the pastor is not bound to an external judicatory. Therefore, the internal dynamics of the individual congregation are more a factor in setting the tone of pastoral leadership. Both historically and currently in the African American independent church, the minister envisioned the direction of the church, was the spokesman for the congregation, and was a respected leader in the African American community. This leadership style is often a source of conflict in connectional churches where decision making is largely the function of laity and is tied to standards set forth by the judicatory and its governance. There are instances in which an African American pastor of a connectional church may adopt the leadership style of the independent pastor. Park Avenue United Methodist Church is an example of this kind of culture clash.

Park Avenue, in a small western city, is in the midst of a demographically changing neighborhood. With a long history in the community, at its peak it had a significant European American membership, some having belonged for 50 or 60 years. In the 1980s the bishop appointed the congregation's first African American pastor. This pastor believed in a strong outreach program and a social gospel, and was very active in the community (for example, starting a community clothes closet for the homeless). The result of the pastor's outreach and community involvement was a significant increase in the number of people of color (Latino, West Indian, Filipino, African American) who joined the congregation. He was also recognized by the city for his efforts on behalf of the community. His leadership style reflected that of the independent church minister. The pastor saw himself as providing the kind of leadership the church needed; the white members, however, saw him as overbearing and dictatorial.

The white members of the congregation had difficulty in adjusting to the pastor, his leadership style, and the new members he recruited.

The pastor's preaching was also a mystery to the white congregants. The preaching style of many African American pastors is to repeat phrases for emphasis. The white members did not understand his apparent need to repeat himself in his sermons. What was a cultural norm in one community was a source of confusion and a catalyst for conflict in another. In their dissatisfaction, the white members began to withdraw from the Sunday morning worship service and organized an alternative Friday service.

Another source of conflict may be the degree to which African American parishioners have assimilated into the dominant white culture. When the survival of a congregation may be at stake, particularly if it is in a transitional neighborhood (white to black), it may begin to struggle with its sense of identity as well as with ways to draw people from the neighborhood. The more assimilated worshipers may more strongly identify with the white denomination and may react negatively to traditional African American gospel music or the introduction of an African American pastor. A conflict can arise between those who want to emulate the European American style of worship and those who want a worship service more reflective of African American culture and which they hope will attract members of the surrounding community. Grove Street Presbyterian Church exemplifies this dynamic.

Grove Street is a small, predominantly African American congregation in a large midwestern city. It is housed in a large edifice that once held over 1,000 worshipers. In the formerly all-white church, over the past three decades membership declined significantly as a casualty of white flight from the inner city to the suburbs. A little over 100 African American parishioners remained. At the time, the surrounding neighborhood was undergoing a major revitalization with an ever-increasing influx of middle-class African American people moving into the area. This presented both a challenge and an opportunity for the church in terms of its mission.

Over 20 years earlier, the senior pastor of Grove Street, a European American, had died in a drowning accident. At the time of his death, the church was fairly even in numbers of African American and European American parishioners. When I was called in, there were only seven European Americans in a congregation of 100 members. Some of the African American members still insisted that the church was wholly integrated. Others wanted to identify the church as being African American. This change created a measure of uncertainty concerning the church's mission. Further complicating this issue was the adulation conferred upon the deceased former pastor. Frequently, he was spoken of in glowing terms and his tenure as a kind of golden age.

There was also a rather heated debate with respect to what kind of music should be played. One group felt the church should keep its paid soloists who sang European sacred music; others felt that a voluntary gospel choir would do more to attract the influx of African Americans in the neighborhood. Some members felt that those who rejected the introduction of African American gospel music identified too strongly with the European American style of worship. This dispute over music was a manifestation of the larger question of identity: "What kind of culture should we reflect, African American or European American?"

RACE

To ignore the significance of race in African American congregations is to ignore the elephant standing in the middle of the room. Although a conflict may not be race based, it has been my experience that a perception of racism, bigotry, or bias is just as significant as its actual presence. Sometimes amidst accelerated tensions and emotions, it is difficult to distinguish the perception from reality. Even in those connectional congregations that are predominantly African American, the question of race is an underlying subtext that bubbles to the surface.

Either directly or indirectly, race is too often the silent participant in a conflict, particularly for churches in transition. Concerns related to the church's mission, dwindling coffers, declining membership, and changing community demographics all tend to exacerbate hidden racial tensions. In mixed congregations (African American and European American) where whites hold the reins of power, they may be accused of engaging in racist behavior. White members may be hesitant to reach out to a community of strangers. They may withhold funds, stop attending worship services, encourage the closing of the church, or demand a change of pastors if the pastor is African American. If the African Americans in the congregation support the pastor and want to expand the church's community outreach, they could find themselves in conflict with their white counterparts. In some cases when African Americans are new to the church, they may have little influence or power.

This was true at Park Avenue United Methodist. The long-time white parishioners withheld their money, withdrew from the Sunday worship service, and demanded a change of pastors. The newer members who were primarily people of color supported the pastor but were not able to sustain the church financially and had very little influence or power because they did not serve on any of the church's boards. The question of why the white members felt a need to organize an alternative worship service, and did not invite any people of color was viewed by some members as an act of racial prejudice.

As stated earlier, the perception of racism is almost as powerful as its reality. There was an incident at Park Avenue in which an African American woman accused an older white woman of racism. The church had a nursery that had an age limit of five years. The white woman had a granddaughter who was eight years old and permitted in the nursery. The African American woman tried to put her six-year-old in the nursery, was reminded of the age limit, and not permitted to put her child in the nursery. When she heard of the European American woman's granddaughter's placement in the nursery, she felt she was a victim of racism. The European American woman explained to me that her granddaughter had developmental disabilities. This information was unknown to the African American woman, whose perception of racism was as powerful as its reality would have been with respect to exacerbating conflict.

CONFLICT MANAGEMENT RESPONSES

The conflict management process is a difficult and delicate one. Mitigating factors, such as sabotage or the removal of the pastor before the conflict is resolved, can derail the process. Successful conflict management also depends on the desire and efforts of all participants to follow through. My work with the aforementioned churches met with varying degrees of resolution.

High Street Lutheran: Based on interviews with the pastor, church leaders, and members, my recommendations included: (1) that High Street revisit its mission with respect to the primarily African American surrounding neighborhood; (2) that they begin a discussion of the impact of race on the congregation; and (3) that they discuss the relationship between the pastor and the congregation. In the midst of the conflict, however, the senior pastor was making covert plans to leave for another pastorate. Although the pastor did transfer to another congregation, the report I submitted provided information that facilitated a smoother transition for the next pastor.

Park Avenue United Methodist: Recommendations to Park Avenue included: (1) an open dialogue between the pastor and the congregation about his leadership; and (2) beginning a discussion between the older European American congregation and the newer members of color. Here, too, the conflict management process was aborted when the pastor was transferred to another congregation. This denied the congregation the opportunity to have an honest dialogue about the role race played in the particular conflict and in the church's life in general. Because the pastor's transfer suggested to them that they had lost, the members of color chose not to attend a meeting that had been organized to talk with the older white members about the racial issues. This short-circuiting of the conflict management process left the door open for potentially incendiary future conflict. Additionally, Park Avenue's unwillingness to address the very crucial issue of race and cultural diversity threatens its long-term survival. It could go the way of many congregations in transitional neighborhoods: dying because it has little promise of attracting new members.

Grove Street Presbyterian: I suggested that the congregation (1) identify issues regarding how members viewed the pastor's performance and how he viewed his performance; (2) work together to decide whether or not the pastor should stay; and (3) identify types of behavior that fostered conflict. As a result, the pastor and congregation decided to continue their relationship and developed a list of mutually agreed-upon expectations. They also drew up a list of healthy conflict management norms, and adopted new behaviors that would improve communication and discourage conflict. These new goals were to be listed in the bulletin every Sunday, thus enculturating them into the life of the church. With respect to the issue of gospel versus traditional music, the congregation reached a compromise. They organized an earlier 8:00 A.M. service that would feature traditional African American gospel music.

Obviously, the varying levels of success in addressing conflicts in these congregations suggest the complexity of the issues involved. Church leadership—bishops, executive ministers, committee heads, and others—must be willing to commit financial and spiritual resources to local congregations dealing with the issues of race, culture, and power as much as they would support a local congregation's building program. This may mean bringing in outside help to assist the church in sorting out the issues engendered by such conflicts and developing long-term solutions. Such support will strengthen not only local congregations, but the church as a whole. It will hasten the establishment of the dominion of God on earth.

Originally published in Congregations: The Alban Journal *24, no. 3 (May/June 1998): pp. 15-18.*

CHAPTER 16

From Surgery to Acupuncture
An Alternative Approach to
Managing Church Conflict from
An Asian American Perspective

Virstan B. Y Choy

Wanting to explore the theme "Improving Harmony and Communication in the Church," an Asian American congregation invites a white counselor to be the keynote speaker for its annual all-members' retreat. The speaker focuses one of the sessions on intergenerational communication.

To encourage openness in sharing, the speaker asks the youth present to identify issues about which they and their parents disagree. No youth responds. The speaker rearranges her audience, asking the adults to sit on one side of the room and the youth to sit on the other. She then rephrases the question to the youth, "Think about the last time you and your parents had an argument. What was it about?" Still no youth responds.

One of the adults new to the congregation tries to help. "Maybe the youth need more time to think up some things to say. Maybe they need anonymity. How about if we break up into two groups—one for the youth, one for the adults—for the next half-hour so that each generation can come up with a list of what bugs them about the other generation. Each group could choose its own reporter so that we won't know who actually made the complaint in the first place." The retreat leader agrees with the suggestion. The members divide into the two groups and meet.

Thirty minutes later, the groups return to the plenary room. The youth are given the opportunity to report first. Their designated reporter reads from a small piece of paper, "As the youth generation of this church, we appreciate the opportunity to share our opinions at this retreat. However, what our parents and we disagree about—well, we don't feel it's right to bring that up in public. We love our parents. What we argue about is between us." She looks to the other youth. They nod in agreement. She turns back to the audience, says "Thank you," and returns to her seat.

A CASE STORY ON FACING CONFLICTS IN A PUBLIC MEETING

In an Asian American congregation, a lay leader is aware of a conflict among some of the members and is unsure about how to respond. She consults a member of her denomination's regional staff, who offers to visit the church and to engage the members in some conflict resolution exercises. In his visit with the congregation, the denominational executive emphasizes "openness in communication" and encourages members to come forward so that, "face-to-face," they might "openly confront" their problems. He asks the members to devote the day-long open meeting to the practice of conflict resolution techniques "effective in other churches that have experienced conflict."

The church members dutifully cooperate with their executive, participating in activities engaging them in presenting their "side" of the issue, answering his questions about background history, and in trying exercises in open communication.

At the end of this process, he presents to the congregation his "findings," his analysis of the conflict based upon these findings, and his recommendations for what the congregation needs to do. One of the findings is the revelation that there is more than one conflict in the congregation, that some members reported disagreements with other members that have existed for over two decades—disagreements "allowed" to remain unresolved. Included in this report is his "power analysis" of the congregation, revealing his perceptions of how power and authority have been skewed in favor of the older generations of the church for over two decades and how dysfunctional it would be for the congregation not to change such a situation. The executive then lists the changes that need to be made in order for the members to resolve their conflicts and to move forward together. He concludes his report by noting the positive results of confronting conflict and the importance of continuing such a "face-to-face" process. He thanks the congregation for its cooperation. The members thank the executive for his time and efforts and close with prayers for him and the church.

The day after this meeting, citing the statements about one another made in public the day before, many of the members announce their decision to leave the congregation.

FROM A HUMAN RELATIONS MODEL TO A
PRESERVING RELATIONSHIPS UNDERSTANDING

Most current approaches to church conflict management are based upon conceptions of congregations as organizations (and congregational leadership as organizational leadership). These conceptions have been primarily shaped by human relations theory. The preceding stories of two actual cases in Asian American congregations show how such approaches are influenced by a psychological understanding of relationships within congregations, which encourages confrontation of disagreements, engages the persons involved in a conflict in direct interaction, and emphasizes communication skills (self-disclosure, assertiveness in expressing demands, negotiation, compromise, and collaboration). The use of such approaches to conflict in Asian American congregations has not been effective.

To understand why, it is helpful to refer to Asian and Asian American researchers (several are listed in the "Selected Resources" section at the end of this article) who remind us that, for Asians, society is not individual-based, but relationship-based. This focus upon relationships is rooted in Confucianism, in which human beings are expected to develop and conduct themselves as "relation-oriented" individuals. Accordingly, attitudes that enable and sustain this relational orientation are cultivated in the Asian family and Asian community. Three such attitudes or relational postures are:

- continuous awareness of one's networks of relationships
- recognition of the importance of "face" (public self-image) for those with whom one is in relationship
- fulfillment of the obligations involved in maintaining one's relationships

These attitudes and postures continue to shape behavior, not just for the immigrant Asian generation as it arrives in this country, but for the American-born generations as well—even to the third and fourth generations. They are predispositional in nature—so influential that they are perceived by some Asian Americans as a sort of "cultural DNA"—not always consciously present, but functionally operative in predisposing Asian Americans to a distinctive posture for engaging in interpersonal interactions in the family, in the community, and in the congregation.

At first look, approaches to congregational conflict emphasizing human relations theory and process might seem consistent with and appropriate to the relational orientation of people belonging to Asian American congregations. Yet, from the perspective of many Asian Americans, the confrontational processes and techniques used in human relations approaches actually violate the cultural values and norms regarding relationship, face, and obligation at the root of their understanding of human relationships. For many Asian Americans, behavior is based not primarily upon one's own feelings, interests, and motivations (as emphasized in the majority American society), but rather upon those of the persons with whom one has relationship. A cultural collision occurs when persons acting out of this posture are placed in conflict management situations emphasizing attention to one's own feelings and calling for expression (and negotiation) of one's own needs and interests. Sensitivity to the following key factors may lead to more effective response to conflict in Asian American congregations:

- the power of the relational orientation
- the predisposition toward preserving relationship
- the preference for nonconfrontational interaction
- the paradox of solidarity in the midst of conflict

The Power of the Relational Orientation

Relationship (rather than individual needs or interests) is at the center of the Asian American orientation to conflict. As reflected in the first case story, this relational orientation influences interpersonal behavior in conflict or potential conflict situations. Understanding this orientation is therefore foundational to the development of any culturally relevant conflict management approaches for Asian Americans.

The Predisposition toward Preserving Relationship

In situations of conflict, the relational orientation leads to a predisposition toward preserving relationship with those with whom one is involved in a disagreement. Consequently, as reflected in the second case story, differences and even disagreements may be allowed to remain unresolved over a long period of time in order to preserve the face of others ("save face") and therefore maintain some form of relationship ("save relationship"). In such situations, what non-Asian American conflict managers may perceive as passivity or inability to make decisions may actually be an intentional, culturally shaped decision not to engage in interactions that threaten face or confrontations which jeopardize relationships.

The Preference for Nonconfrontational Interaction

In face-to-face interactions between Person A and Person B, there are four possible outcomes: A might lose face, B might lose face, both A and B might lose face, neither A nor B might lose face. Since three of the four possibilities result in loss of face, the odds do not favor a face-saving outcome in most processes calling for face-to-face interactions! Consequently, the predisposition toward preserving relationships leads to the preference for nonconfrontational interaction. This is not a preference for inactivity, but for active nonconfrontation in conflict interactions with one another. Such nonconfrontation takes the form of subtle or indirect engagement of parties in disagreement, for instance, through trusted third-party "go-betweens" who serve as avenues for indirect communication (rather than professional mediators who engage disputants in direct communication).

The Paradox of Solidarity in the Midst of Conflict

The predisposition toward preserving relationships enables the toleration of ambiguity in these relationships in times of disagreement. Some Asian American congregations have remained together in the midst of their differences, deferring debate or other open efforts designed to resolve the dispute. Some Asian Americans have characterized such congregational cohesion in the face of conflict as "solidarity in conflict" in contrast to the "unity in diversity" emphasized in some mainline denominations. This difference has theological implications: How might a theology of solidarity be different from a theology of unity or a theology of reconciliation in shaping our conflict ministry?

From Surgery to Acupuncture

In addressing problems in interpersonal and intergroup relationships, many Asian Americans are inclined to adopt a posture of subtlety, indirectness, and nonconfrontational interaction. They are not inclined to adopt most current approaches to church conflict management, which involve direct, face-to-face interactions, personal disclosures in public settings, as well as provision of private personal information to outsiders or strangers. Like surgery, these approaches involve cutting the body open, exposing for examination (and therefore exposing to risk) delicate parts of the body, and sometimes even cutting and removal of parts of the body. Like surgery, such techniques are invasive. Like surgery, they risk causing trauma to the body. Like surgery, they sometimes cause the death of the body.

In contrast, acupuncture is less invasive, less incising, and less risky. Rather than pre-surgery X-rays, probes, or the introduction of other foreign chemicals or instruments into the body, it involves noninvasive external observation of key points of the body. Rather than involving surgical incisions, this approach calls only for the gentle insertion of small needles. Rather than identifying, examining, chemically treating and/or cutting out parts of the body, acupuncture seeks to keep body parts in healthy relation to one another, working to free the flow of energy within the body and between its parts. For many Asian Americans, acupuncture is an attractive metaphor suggesting new ways of intervening in church conflicts.

Given its emphasis upon maintaining balance in the body and enabling the free flow of energy within the body, the acupuncture metaphor provides an opportunity for reconceiving intervention, mediation, and the use of third-party consultants in conflict situations. Consultants need a posture less like that of an "outside expert" in objective process and more like an intermediary—not necessarily mediator nor arbitrator, but more a "go-between" who provides an avenue for subtle and indirect contact between people in conflict. A "shadow consultant" who works informally in the background rather than directly and visibly may provide the sort of noninvasive intervention suggested by the acupuncture image.

SOME QUESTIONS FOR RESPONDING TO
ASIAN AMERICAN CONFLICT

For people seeking to utilize the observations and proposals in this essay, the following questions may be of help. They are offered, not as a new protocol to be followed for an Asian American conflict, but as questions to be asked in an acupuncture posture or spirit by those working with Asian American congregations.

Assessment of a Conflict Situation

1. In what ways is ethnicity a factor in this congregation? How has such ethnicity been a factor during times of previous conflict?
2. In what ways are the four key factors and dynamics affecting Asian American conflict present and operative in this congregation?
3. How does the culture of the congregation's members provide ways for people in conflict to manage or resolve their differences? Which of those ways are operative in this congregation?
4. To what extent does the congregation already use third parties or "go-betweens" in interpersonal interactions, decision making, conflict? How have they been helpful in the past in this congregation?

Developing a Response to a Conflict Situation

5. In a conflict situation, what might constitute an "acupuncture-like" approach to responding?
6. Given the "energy flow" image in the acupuncture metaphor, how is the energy flow of the congregation at this point? What keeps it flowing? Is there any blockage? What is needed to "unblock" the energy flow?
7. If "go-betweens" are used, are any "available" (willing) to assist in enabling nonconfrontational communication and interaction between the parties in the conflict?
8. How might a shadow consultant be acceptable and used in this conflict?

CONCLUSION

The five key factors in Asian American conflict and the proposal for an acupuncture-like approach presented here represent initial discoveries on the path to a culturally sensitive approach to conflict management in Asian American congregations. Such a proposal does not represent a dismissal of existing approaches by church consultants and denominational executives. It does represent an alert to the limits and liabilities of approaches based upon one particular understanding of human relationships and the conception of interpersonal interactions following from it. In addition, this proposal may not be limited to use in Asian American churches. Just as some Western medical practitioners have become open to the appropriateness and benefits of acupuncture for certain health problems, leaders of congregations seeking alternatives to surgery-like conflict management processes may want to explore acupuncture-like approaches.

SELECTED RESOURCES

Augsburger, David. *Conflict Mediation across Cultures: Pathways and Patterns.* Louisville: Westminster John Knox, 1992.

Kendis, Kaoru Oguri. *A Matter of Comfort: Ethnic Maintenance and Ethnic Style among Third-Generation Japanese Americans.* New York: AMS Press, Inc., 1989.

King, Ambrose Yeo-chi. "Kuan-Hsi and Network Building: A Sociological Interpretation." In "The Living Tree: The Changing Meaning of Being Chinese Today." *Daedalus* 120, no. 2 (Spring, 1991): pp. 63-84.

Lebra, Takie Sugiyama. "Nonconfrontational Strategies for Management of Interpersonal Conflicts." In *Conflict in Japan,* ed. E. S. Krauss, T. P. Rohlen, P. G. Steinhoff. Honolulu: University of Hawaii Press, 1984. Pp. 41-60.

Perrow, Charles. *Complex Organizations: A Critical Essay.* 3rd ed. New York: McGraw-Hill, 1986.

Originally published in Congregations: The Alban Journal *21, no. 6 (November/ December 1995): pp. 16-19.*

CHAPTER 17

Teach Us to Needle, Needle Us to Learn

A Response to Virstan Choy's "From Surgery to Acupuncture"

David W. Augsburger

Virstan B. Y. Choy has pricked our over-inflated trust in direct, dialogical, open-system processes for resolving conflict. He has almost painlessly needled the swollen cultural egos that assume multicultural applicability to Western theories (which don't work that well for us, we Westerners might admit). He has practiced the same acupuncture in his tactful writing, which, as he observes, is necessary in Asian conflict resolution.

He has inserted long—very long—needles that reach to several of the Western basic assumptions that lie deep in our social and personal psyches. He has nudged our neural nodes to let go, let be, and let ourselves see other visions.

Western conflict assumptions—basic assumptions that lie beneath the theory and practice of conflict interventions—are commonly shaped by three metaphors: War, sports, and business. In war, survival is at stake, is everything. In sports, achievement is central, winning is everything. In business, profit is the bottom line, success is all. Inevitably, the other party in the conflict will be seen as an opponent who must be conquered, a heretic who must be silenced, an enemy who must be excluded, a devil who must be destroyed.

All conflicts, in this dualistic vision, are either competitive or collaborative, destructive or constructive, malignant or benign (see the works of Morton Deutsch, Rollo May, and Erich Fromm). When we split all conflict into two types, we get seduced into "either/or" thinking. We split from others because we are splitting inside. We fragment in the face of conflict and our thinking becomes more concrete, more polarized, more divisive. We are divided selves. In the end, disputes are "either-or" dilemmas. Either we will win or lose, live or die.

Where the West is *either/or*, the Asian world begins from *both/and*. Harmony and solidarity are central values that presuppose complementarity. In the Indic and African worlds, there are many groups that prefer a third option—*neither/nor*. Neither party is assumed right, neither will win. Instead the community will create a solution that resolves the dispute and that they—not the disputants—own. The three options—competition, complementarity, or creativity—offer deeply contrasting outcomes even as they begin from very different basic assumptions. Of course, mediators in every culture make use of all three approaches, but the starting point, the dominant process, the preferred outcome are strongly shaped by the primary metaphor.

Westerners *feel* better when the parties in a dispute are talking openly again; Westerners are *more comfortable* when the issues are named, defined, placed on the table by both sides; Westerners trust direct negotiations, immediate conversations, candid exploration, mutual/authentic/vulnerable give-and-take; Westerners relax as resolution moves toward face-to-face reconciliation symbolized by a handshake or a hug. These are signs that constructive, collaborative, benign processes are being used to choose the *right* outcome in the *right* way (for the vindication of those who are right).

"Ultimately we must choose; finally someone must yield; eventually the right will prevail." Westerners believe in deeply held cultural myths of the righteous individual triumphing over the evil conspiracy. Of course, there are multiple myths, varied assumptions, diverse expectations, but communal solidarity is feared as cultic or is left to the Amish and the triumph of the majority is the best we can hope for. Surgery is necessary. Amputation may be regrettably required. A transplant (get rid of the old leadership and import the new) may be the only way to save lives. And since Western know-how is better, other groups (especially those who are nondominant cultures within our world because they are not like us) should learn our conflict theory, profit from our research, gain from our wisdom ("Scratch any person in the world and under the surface there's an American trying to get out," imperialism teaches us.)

Not only do distinctive Hispanic, Arabic, Indian, Asian, and African American conflict patterns differ sharply from the dominant Western models, they have much to teach us. The exchange is clearly mutual, two-way, with equal contributions to make. In conflict theory, the playing field is far more level than we have been able or willing to see.

Virstan Choy, writing to Asian and Asian American congregations, offers a clear challenge to Western models: prizing relationship, seeking to preserve relational integrity, utilizing the predisposition toward harmony and solidarity, and utilizing the polarities and the paradoxes of solidarity to work out the tensions in relationship and the contrasts in goals creatively.

The metaphor of acupuncture is intriguing and at the same time illuminatingly clear. In acupuncture, one deciphers the energy flow, identifies the nodal trigger points, and makes an invisible intervention. Skilled leadership in conflict situations can take clear nonanxious positions with the right people in the system to activate positive cycles of change. Rather than raising the anxiety in the system, as Kurt Lewin has taught us, this reduces it by gently removing a block or reducing a drive. Third-party processes become the art of making new connections, disconnecting old binds and bonds.

Carl Whitaker, the family therapist, once likened his work to the miming of Charlie Chaplin. When he was young, he danced with the footwork of a genius, but as he grew old, Chaplin, the little clown, became a minimalist. Gone were the steps and the flowing gestures. Instead, everything could be said by bowing the head and lightly lifting the hat. "What I do in therapy, as I grow older," Whitaker said, "is like Chaplin's simple gesture. I want to forget the footwork and learn when to lift my hat."

That is acupuncture. To know the trigger point. To release the nervous energy. To heal.

Lead on, Asian churches. Lead on in your own unique wisdom on the healing process. Lead out in this challenging other groups' assumptions through kind of dialogue. Our surgery has not been all that successful. We have much to learn.

Originally published in Congregations: The Alban Journal *22, no. 1 (January/ February 1996): pp. 18-19.*

CHAPTER 18

Making My World View Visible
A Response to Virstan Choy's
"From Surgery to Acupuncture"

Alice Mann

Virstan Choy, in his essay on church conflict "from an Asian American perspective" (chapter 16) makes several important contributions to the field of congregation development. Most directly, he provides some possible criteria for deciding what kinds of assistance might be appropriate for congregations rooted in Asian cultures. Choy urges the use of methods that acknowledge this group's:

- relational orientation;
- predisposition toward preserving relationship; preference for nonconfrontational interaction; and,
- capacity for solidarity in the face of conflict.

Such guidance helps pastors, consultants, and denominational staff to respond better to specific cultural environments. But Choy's work raises (in my mind) larger issues than "proper techniques" for Asian American congregations. I'd like to identify three important conversations that might grow out of Choy's observations.

1. *We need to set in cultural context the entire body of knowledge about congregation development.* When I tell a group "what the literature says" or "what we know" about conflict resolution, a whole reef of questions lies hidden below the surface of my statements. What culture has generated the ideas I am presenting? What historical period do they reflect? What sources of wisdom have been honored and ignored in constructing those ideas? Which voices have established the terms of the conversation, and which have been relegated to the status of "others"?

Virstan Choy challenges me as a practitioner to note the cultural context of my own assertions and to avoid a stance equivalent to the "omniscient narrator" in literature—a disembodied voice that purports to reveal what is really happening in this situation and these characters. During my stint as a graduate student in English, I was especially grateful to the novelist Russell Banks for his insistence that a white author is obligated to make visible in her work the racial and ethnic components (and limitations) of her own world view. I find myself wondering now how this same ethical commitment can be reflected in the work of congregation development— how the "unmarked" categories (white, European American, middle class) can carry their proper labels, so that I do not present myself as the "omniscient narrator" of a multicultural story, a reality that cannot be fully described from a single frame of reference.

2. *"Cultural differences" between men and women might be explored in relation to Virstan Choy's criteria.* The work of researchers like Deborah Tannen suggests that distinctive male and female subcultures may interact to create the larger "culture" of a people. Some would say that women (or should we say "white middle-class women in the U.S."?) tend to emphasize the relational in their communication patterns. If this is so, we might find some common ground between Asian American voices and feminist/womanist voices in the church.

I would proceed cautiously, however, in defining what that common ground might be. American women of European background may tend to worry about preserving relationships more than our male counterparts do— but we both have a narrow, atomistic definition of "relationship" compared to men and women from cultures with a livelier sense of communal identity.

3. *"Mainstream churches" may be challenged by Asian American congregations to reassess the relative value of disclosure and privacy.* Choy's work sheds new light for me on the current preoccupation—both in the wider culture and in religious systems—with disclosure as opposed to privacy. Following Barry Johnson and others, we might identify disclosure and privacy as a "polarity"—a creative tension between opposites—which must be managed rather than resolved in order for a community to remain healthy. A polarity resembles a set of scales tipping back and forth between two "weighty" values. What I learned from Choy's essay is that the fulcrum (or balancing post) of the scale doesn't fall in the same place for every culture because the "good" at one end may not be given exactly the same weight as the "good" at the other end.

Privacy (or "personal space") is a positive value, to be held in tension with self-disclosure (or transparency, or "openness") for the health of persons and communities. The downside of privacy—secrecy—seems at the moment to be condemned as the cardinal sin in mainstream American culture, and for some good reasons. Secrecy tends to favor and perpetuate existing power structures. The illegitimate power of Iran-Contra conspirators depended on secrecy, and so does the tyranny of a parent (or pastor) who is sexually abusing a child.

On the other hand, we can see the downside of exposure in the emotional "feeding frenzy" that occurs when authority figures (civil servants, parents, clergy) are accused of serious violations of trust. Churches will pay a high price in the long run if we remain in that mode regarding clergy sexual abuse—if, for example, judicatory materials on clergy background checks express an appropriately high concern for the person reporting abuse, but do not articulate a similar commitment to due process for an accused person. We can also see the destructive side of exposure in the format of the less responsible talk shows, where traumatized people are encouraged to tell all for the sake of public entertainment and private profit. Choy's discussion of "face" may help the rest of us do some reevaluation of the way we deal with matters involving shame. If we listen to our own imagery (red-faced, egg on the face, slap in the face), we will discover that concern with "face" is not unique to Asian cultures. From listening to others who weigh these competing "goods" somewhat differently, we might gain greater perspective on our current choices, and swing less recklessly from cover-up to witch-hunt and back again.

Originally published in Congregations: The Alban Journal *22, no. 1 (January/February 1996): pp. 19-20.*

CHAPTER 19

Mediation:
What Can We Learn from the Chinese?

Margaret E. Bruehl

In May of 1989, I spent three weeks in China, as a delegate representing the Alban Institute, with the People to People Citizen Ambassador Program. The delegation was invited by the Chinese Ministry of Justice to engage in a professional exchange with lawyers, judges, and mediators. Our focus was to examine alternate dispute-resolution techniques practiced in the People's Republic of China. As an Alban consultant I was most interested in the mediation that took place with families, in neighborhoods, and at the work place, and the potential application for our churches.

I was surprised to discover that while China's Community Mediation system has its roots in ancient community traditions, it has become an increasingly important component in the nation's legal system over the years. Mediation, rather than litigation, is the prevailing method of dispute resolution. The mediation system operates under the direction of the Ministry of Justice, which has a department in each province or city that is responsible for setting guidelines for the committees and is advised and aided by legal assistants and the courts of law.

The provincial departments give assistance in setting up work groups (the Mediation Committees), in establishing procedures, and in training mediators. They encourage mediators to exchange information and they praise their "good work and good deeds." They help them analyze how disputes arise and inform them on what tendencies to expect. For example, crowded living conditions create many disputes about use of kitchen and toilet facilities. Mid-summer is a peak period for disputes between neighbors because of the large numbers of persons congregating outdoors. The style of the mediator may be very informal, as in carrying a message between two feuding neighbors, or quite formal, as when someone submits an application to an elected municipal People's Mediation Committee, which must be followed up by contacting the involved parties to determine whether they are amenable to mediation. Mediation is voluntary, and thus must be agreed on.

Chinese mediation practice is based on a value system tied to a deep respect for family—especially elders—to the acceptance of authority, and to holding an obligation to that authority in their culture. Each neighborhood community, village, and urban district has a Mediation Committee, as do the social and political organizations, enterprises, and factories. In 1989, mediators numbered 6.2 million in the country. This provides a network of mediators throughout China that is convenient to the people in all settings and areas of life.

Chinese mediation emphasizes harmony, upholding of good morals, maintaining a good attitude, knowing the difference between right and wrong, being correct, and saving face. Disharmony is not only a reflection on the parties engaged in a dispute but also on their families; it is thought to be a comment on their inability to conform to the behavioral norms that are the unifying substance of Chinese society.

American culture functions differently. By contrast, we emphasize privacy and individual rights rather than collective rights. Families are frequently scattered or are loosely connected. Members of congregations attend their churches for a variety of reasons and they alone determine their degree of participation, interaction, and contribution. In light of these and other cultural differences, is the potential for using the Chinese mediation process for dispute resolution in our congregations limited or impossible?

In China, mediators are a work unit. The qualifications for selection are fairness, patience, sincerity, and warm-heartedness. They are expected to have good relations with people, to love mediation work, and to have some knowledge of the law. Most are workers or neighborhood people who work on a voluntary basis, and committees usually consist of three to 11 persons.

Can we consider such a work unit in our congregations—an elected committee requiring similar qualifications for selection? For example, could small groups of persons, trained in mediation skills, manage some internal congregational problems and grievances? I am intrigued with the possibility of using such a group of elected, respected persons to act as bridge builders, mediators, troubleshooters, and teachers in congregational settings. These persons could be expected to have an interest in people and in relations between and among people, to take training in mediation skills and methods, and to have a knowledge of the denominational structure and law that governs their church. Could competent trainees accept such a responsibility? Would parishioners be open to using such a service?

Before taking on the responsibility either to train as a mediator or to accept the help of one, parishioners would need to know what a mediator does. In summary, the mediator is an acceptable, impartial third party with no authoritative decision-making power. The mediator assists persons who are in disagreement or tension with one another, or who are involved in disputes, to reach mutually agreeable solutions. There are two stages to the mediation process. In the first stage, prior to joint mediation sessions, the mediator explores the situation with the individual persons involved, describes the mediator's role and function, and determines with the individuals an agreeable approach for how they will handle the difficulty. A decision to work with the mediator is construed as a first agreement, and a time and place is mutually determined for the next step in the mediation process. It is important in this premediation stage to build credibility as a neutral facilitator, to clarify the sequence of steps that will be used in mediation, and to practice conciliation—aimed at correcting perception, reducing unreasonable fears, and improving communication so that reasonable discussion can take place when the individuals meet together. Patience and focus are essential.

During the second stage, the mediator explains how the mediation process will take place, including the use of separate caucus sessions as a normal procedure (for instance, when a time to vent feelings is needed or to test potential agreements) and possibly setting guidelines for behavior during mediation sessions (for instance, having one person speak at a time or asking questions for clarification only). Following the preparation period, the mediator assists the parties in beginning productive negotiation by identifying the important issues and building an agenda for discussion. Interests are identified that underlie the positions either of the individuals has taken, and conciliation practices continue. Once that has been accomplished, options for solution are invented and then assessed. Finally, the interacting parties make decisions that take each of their needs into account. In mediation training, each step of this process is developed and practiced.

Position	Interest
1. The choir director should be fired.	1. We never hear any of the old hymns at our service. I'd like that as part of my worship experience.
2. I won't serve on a committee chaired by him/her.	2. I don't feel listened to or re-spected by him/her. In fact, I'm intimidated because of how I often was interrupted and talked over in our last work experience.
3. The new secretary isn't as efficient as the last one.	3. The new secretary doesn't do things like they used to be done. I used to hear from the pastor the same day I called, without even having to ask.

The effect of persons holding opposite positions and operating out of such a context often leads to interpersonal conflicts and to church fights. Rumors circulate, grievances abound, and sometimes factions form.

How and why might mediation committees be helpful? We must live with differences because there are many. We can ignore them, resent them, squabble over them, or work with them. Differing interests sometimes block our ability to work together, to be good neighbors, and can lead to win/lose conflicts. These are frequently signs of low-level conflict that need not escalate to high levels. The use of mediation can provide a way to manage our differences if we remember four key elements:

1. Promptness—get there at the first alarm
2. Stability—keep it cool
3. Mediation—help resolve the difficulty
4. Contact—have a return visit with the party or parties

This is how Chinese abbreviate mediation steps:

1. Separate the disputing parties ("Birds want to sing at the same time")
2. Listen to each of them; get their side of the story
3. Extinguish the emotional fire
4. Mediate
5. Have a return visit; check in to see if their agreements are working and continue to give them care and concern

In Nanjing, a Mediation Committee Director of a 12-building apartment complex offered this advice to us:

> To do mediation you need the whole: sincerity, warmth, fairness, patience.
>
> Use your mind—think,
> > your legs—go to them,
> > your mouth—talk to them.
>
> Persuade—use humor, reasoning to cool the case down.
>
> Show your love; show your hard edges and softness.
>
> You need to have a quick mind, find the right time to break the defense line (the position?) of the party if it is there.
>
> Levelheadedness and patience are required—you can't get into a quarrel with the parties. You must know the law.
>
> You must practice in your life the good relationships you try to uphold in mediation.
>
> As a mediator, problems will come to you. If you choose to do this, be prepared for hard work.

Is it possible or feasible to use mediation as a means of promoting greater interpersonal understanding, to resolve disagreements, to reduce tension and dysfunctional conflict to a creative, problem-solving level? For mediation committees to be of help in our congregations will require the support of both the members and the leadership.

Originally published in Action Information *15, no. 1 (January/February 1989): pp. 8-10.*

David W. Augsburger is professor of pastoral care and counseling at Fuller Theological Seminary in Pasadena, California, and the author of *Conflict Mediation across Cultures* (1995) and *Helping People Forgive* (1996).

Margaret E. Bruehl is an Alban Institute senior consultant emeritus. Her work continues in team building, conflict management, and visioning with Pneuman/Bruehl Associates (419-384-3805/631-751-5099). She lives in Setauket, New York.

Virstan B. Y. Choy is currently General Presbyter for Nurture and Development for the Presbytery of San Francisco, Presbyterian Church (USA). The article "From Surgery to Acupuncture" was written when he was director of field education and integrative studies and associate professor of ministry at San Francisco Theological Seminary. Mr. Choy has previously been a member of the Alban Institute Consulting Network.

Speed B. Leas is an Alban Institute senior consultant and visiting professor of congregational leadership at Pacific School of Religion in Berkeley, California. For over 33 years he has served as a teacher and consultant to ecclesiastical groups throughout the U.S. and Canada, specializing in work with conflicted congregations, judicatories, and church agencies. Among his numerous articles and books are *The Inviting Church: A Study of New Member Assimilation* (1987, with Roy M. Oswald), *Understanding Your Congregation as a System* (1993, with George D. Parsons), and *Moving Your Congregation through Conflict* (1985), all published by the Alban Institute.

David B. Lott, volume editor, is managing editor for the Alban Institute. He received his M.Div. from Luther Seminary in St. Paul, Minnesota, and was an editor with Fortress Press in Minneapolis for over 11 years prior to coming to Alban in 1998. He lives with his cats Natchez and Tujague ("conflict managers *par excellence*") in Washington, D.C.

Alice Mann is an Episcopal priest, has pastored six congregations, and is currently a senior consultant with the Alban Institute, with an emphasis on growth strategies, leadership skills, strategic planning, and spirituality. For two decades she served in the dual roles of local pastor and nationally recognized consultant-trainer in the area of parish development. Her Alban publications include the books *The In-Between Church: Navigating Size Transitions in Congregations* (1998), *Can Our Church Live? Redeveloping Congregations in Decline* (1999), and the video *What Size Should We Be? Visioning the In-Between Church* (2000).

Clinton A. McCoy is the Executive Presbyter of the Presbytery of Northern New York, Presbyterian Church (USA). The father of two grown children, he resides with his wife Barbara in Canton, New York. A fly fisherman and fly tier, he loves the majesty of mountains and sparkle of moving water.

George D. Parsons is a former senior consultant with the Alban Institute, and currently is an organization development consultant who specializes in contention management. He resides in Eugene, Oregon and is the author, with Speed B. Leas, of *Understanding Your Congregation as a System* (Alban, 1993).

Roy W. Pneuman is an Alban Insitute senior consultant emeritus. His work continues in team building, conflict management, and visioning with Pneuman/Bruehl Associates (419-384-3805/631-751-5099). He lives in Pandora, Ohio.

James A. Sparks is emeritus professor of continuing studies and health and human issues, University of Wisconsin, Madison.

Ernest W. Walker is a former consultant with the Alban Institute and is currently the Diversity Programs Coordinator with Alameda County Social Services Agency in Oakland, California. He is a contributing author to the forthcoming book *Leading for Diversity: How School Leaders Promote Positive Interethnic Relations.* He may be contacted at 8822 Dowling St. #B, Oakland, CA, 94605; phone number (510)562-1473.

Caroline A. Westerhoff is the Canon for Congregational Life and Ministry in the Episcopal Diocese of Atlanta. Formerly a senior consultant with the Alban Institute, she has served as assistant to the Bishop of Atlanta; visiting lecturer in religious education at the School of Theology, University of the South; and has had extensive experience as a consultant to congregations, judicatories, and national church organizations. She is the author of *Calling: A Song for the Baptized* (1994) and *Good Fences: The Boundaries of Hospitality* (1999), both published by Cowley Publications. Her third book, *Moments of Revelation: Glimpses Into the Mystery*, is scheduled to be published by The Pilgrim Press in 2002. With her husband, John Westerhoff, she has written two books, *Living Into Our Baptism* and *On the Threshold of God's Future.*

Warner White, a retired parish priest (Episcopal), is a consultant to congregations or judicatories under stress from conflict, the departure of a pastor, a change in leadership styles, and the like. He sings bass in his parish choir and the Burlington (Vermont) Choral Society. He bicycles and is struggling to learn cross-country skiing.